Midlife Investing Strategies:

A Comprehensive Guide to Investing in Your 40s

Table of Contents

Introduction
Chapter 1: Reasons to Invest
Chapter 2: How to Use Your Net Worth to Build Wealth
Chapter 3: A Word About Insurance
Chapter 4: Learning About Equities
Chapter 5: When You Have a Fixed Income
Chapter 6: Investing in Real Estate
Chapter 7: Investing in Commodities
Chapter 8: Cryptocurrencies
Chapter 9: Lesser-Known Investment Opportunities
Chapter 10: Pitfalls to Overcome
Conclusion

© **Copyright 2018 by _____ - All rights reserved.**

The following eBook is reproduced below with the goal of providing information that is as accurate and reliable as possible. Regardless, purchasing this eBook can be seen as consent to the fact that both the publisher and the author of this book are in no way experts on the topics discussed within and that any recommendations or suggestions that are made herein are for entertainment purposes only. Professionals should be consulted as needed prior to undertaking any of the action endorsed herein.

This declaration is deemed fair and valid by both the American Bar Association and the Committee of Publishers Association and is legally binding throughout the United States.

Furthermore, the transmission, duplication or reproduction of any of the following work including specific information will be considered an illegal act irrespective of if it is done electronically or in print. This extends to creating a secondary or tertiary copy of the work or a recorded copy and is only allowed with an expressed written consent from the Publisher. All additional rights reserved.

The information in the following pages is broadly considered to be truthful and accurate account of facts, and as such any inattention, use or misuse of the information in question by the reader will render any resulting actions solely under their purview. There are no scenarios in which the publisher or the original author of this work can be in any fashion deemed liable for any hardship or damages that may befall them after undertaking information described herein.

Additionally, the information in the following pages is intended only for informational purposes and should thus be thought of as universal. As befitting its nature, it is presented without assurance regarding its prolonged validity or interim quality. Trademarks that are mentioned are done without written consent and can in no way be considered an endorsement from the trademark holder.

DOWNLOAD YOUR FREE BONUS:

77 Wealth Secrets

Go to: http://bit.ly/wealthsecrets77

Introduction

Congratulations on downloading *Midlife Investing Strategies: A Comprehensive Guide to Investing in Your 40s*, and thank you for doing so.

Nowadays, it is rare to find anyone who doesn't understand the importance of investing, but when you are young, the urgency of the matter seems to be far off into the future. Ideally, one should start investing in the earlier years of life, but the innocence of youth often gets in the way. It's like when people are warned about impending doom from global warming: it is difficult to grasp a catastrophe that is expected to happen maybe thirty, forty, or fifty years in the future.

To the young, time seems to be ever on their side. Their attention is often focused on getting the best out of life—how to exercise their new chances at independence; learning how to live on their own, experimenting with relationships, traveling, and just plain old adventure seeking. The idea of planning for retirement when you've just landed your first job doesn't seem to fit into their global view of things.

But something happens when you reach your thirties or forties. The seriousness of life begins to take hold. By now, you've got a family, probably a mountain-load of debt, and a host of responsibilities that you have to deal with. The realization probably comes on suddenly. You come home from work, tired and exhausted, and in your attempt to relieve the stress, all those warnings from your parents, teachers, and other advisors come flooding back, completely unbidden.

What am I doing to take care of my family?
How much money do I need to put my children through college?
How am I going to pay my bills if Social Security is not going to be around?
When am I ever going to find the time to see the world—how will I pay for it?

All of a sudden, that dream-like perception of independence and freedom doesn't look so rosy anymore. It has now been clouded with fears about your future. Perhaps you've started some sort of savings account but are slowly beginning to realize that the dismal returns are not enough to keep you in the black as it grows. In fact, it's clear that the scanty interest rates they offer are not even able to keep up with the growing inflation. According to some estimates, with an average 3% inflation rate per year, your $100 will barely buy $22 worth of goods in a few decades.

Your twenties and thirties have taught you that education isn't exclusive to schools and books. Life can teach some pretty hard lessons; it can have any of us putting up a wary defense against all the negative things that could have happened in our past. By the time most people reach their forties, they've learned about divorce, separation, getting fired, getting scammed, and a whole host of other experiences that, over time, temper their enthusiasm and compel them to fall into a life of drudgery.

So, while there may be many young people who launch into the world of investment in their younger years, it seems that by and large, it is in their forties that they finally begin to realize that those good times won't last forever: they need to rethink their approach to prepare for what's coming.

The good news is that, at this point in time, it is perfectly okay to get serious. Jobs become more stable, salaries are better, and, if you've had any kind of financial sense to speak of, monthly obligations are stabilizing. If you could only manage to reign in the credit card spending, you might actually be set for life. It's the perfect time to either start investing or to take your investing approach to the next level.

This is why investing in your forties tends to ensure better results. At this age, people no longer focus on the next big vacation, nor are they interested in the latest fashions. By this time, they've settled down, and most have already started a family of their own. They are grounded and are seriously looking to the future, not just for themselves but also for those they are now responsible for.

Ideally, it is best to start investing earlier. According to some reports, consistently investing in your twenties or thirties will yield more than double the results over those that wait until their forties to begin. This statistic pointed out in Darwin's Finance online magazine, made it clear that if you had contributed $5000 a year between the ages of 25 and 35, you would have yielded more returns than if you had put in $5000 a year between the ages of 35 and 65.

This statement should be a catalyst for anyone interested in developing an investment strategy to start investing now. The longer you wait, the fewer returns you will receive. However, these figures will work with any ten-year timeframe. So, if you have now reached your forties and have yet to start investing, it should emphasize the point that there is no time like the present to get started. With that said, let's start looking at your options now.

DOWNLOAD YOUR FREE BONUS:

77 Wealth Secrets Go to:http://bit.ly/wealthsecrets77

Chapter 1: Reasons to Invest

One of the main reasons so many people put off investing is because they don't know how to do it. It is really sad that after all our years spent getting an education, studying everything from your ABCs to the elements contained on the periodic table, few people really understand the basic concepts involved in making an investment. In fact, many may not even be sure what investing actually is.

The basic concept of investing is to find ways for your money to earn money for you. So, rather than working for forty or fifty years for a minuscule pension, your investments will begin to generate a passive income with minimal input or effort from you. For example, let's say you decided to invest in the stock market and you purchase shares in Starbucks. Ideally, you will watch the market and wait for a drop in value, then purchase the shares and wait for the price to go up. If you sell at that point, then you will have earned a profit.

This is a relatively easy form of investing. However, few people realize that Starbucks also pays a quarterly dividend. So, if you are holding 100 shares of Starbucks, you will receive a small percentage payment for each of those shares, not just once but every quarter, for as long as Starbucks continues to be profitable and you own those shares, which could conceivably amount to much more over the years than you would receive when you buy and sell.

You may have also heard that a good investment option is real estate. Some people simply buy property, renovate, and resell it at a higher price. Others consider renting it out, collecting monthly rents, and hoping it will increase in value over the years. The fact of the matter is, there are hundreds of different directions you can go when it comes to investing. This book is going to look at some of the most common investment strategies used today, but it in no way covers every possibility.

While there is always a certain level of risk associated with investing, it pays to take the time to evaluate your personal reasons to invest before you decide which option will work best for you. The reality is that any type of investing will change in nature over time. A stock that is quickly moving up the charts can suddenly change direction and begin to lose value, a rental property may have to deal with long periods of vacancies, and the bank you are saving with may no longer be able to maintain the interest rate you are currently getting. For those reasons, we'll also discuss the possible risks of investing and how you might protect yourself from them.

On some occasions, an investment you choose could lose its entire value over time, taking all of your money with it. This often happens when a company you hold shares in declares bankruptcy or when your property is destroyed by some type of natural disaster. While negative things like this can and do happen from time to time, it should not be your primary reason for avoiding investing. Change and risk is an unavoidable part of life. People do not avoid living in Florida because they might have to face a hurricane, nor do people avoid going to California because they dread earthquakes. That is because the advantages far outweigh the possible risks. The reality is that there is no way to get the kind of returns on your investments needed without being willing to accept some risks.

However, it is possible to limit your exposure to risk by not getting involved in impulsive investments. To do this, you need to have a good and solid investment plan.

Why Are You Investing?

In creating your personal investment plan, one of the first questions you should ask yourself is why are you investing in the first place. You need to know and understand your ultimate goal—where you want to be financially—and then create the necessary steps to get there. There are probably just as many reasons as there are investors. The decision is based on your personal goals and present circumstances, so no two investment plans are exactly identical. However, some of the most common reasons to invest include:

- Planning for retirement

- Paying for your children's college education
- Creating a life of financial independence
- Traveling
- Pursuing a lifelong dream (climbing Mt. Everest or an around-the-world bike trip)

We've been told for years that relying on a government- or employer-supported pension is not always a practical decision. This is especially true in the USA. As the Baby Boomer generation is entering their retirement years, it is evident that the following generation does not have enough of a workforce to keep the government social security payments going and provide for them. Birthrates have also dropped considerably, and with modern technology and advanced medical practices, people are living longer than previous generations did.

Whatever your plans for the future, it makes sense for you to create some sort of investment plan that will allow you to continue to live a comfortable life without having to depend on such options to sustain you. The sooner you start investing, the more secure your future will be regardless of your reasons.

How Much Return Should You Expect?

Because so many people invest for different reasons, their expectations can also vary. What you can expect from your investments will depend on different circumstances: how risky your investment tool is, how much you put into it, your own personal level of patience. You also have to consider the natural fluctuations of the market. In short, it is impossible to make a general statement that will fit all situations.

It is believed that investing in the stock market can give you an average of 12% return every year, but based on the above variables, that may be true in only some circumstances. It will be up to you to determine how much you should expect to get from your returns.

Let's take stocks, for example. First, when you invest your money in a particular stock, you will notice that the price for each share fluctuates up and down. It is never completely stable. You need to understand why those prices change. When it comes to stock shares there are at least three reasons why the price may go up:

1) There was income earned on the investment in the form of interest, or a dividend was paid.
2) Investments in the company were sold after they appreciated in value (sometimes referred to as a realized gain).
3) The investment went up in value, which basically means that the demand for that particular share increased.

You also need to understand why the price of that stock has decreased in value. Perhaps the demand for those shares waned a bit, or there was a significant amount of debt the company holds.

When investing in the stock market, one thing is painfully clear. A prime reason for why there is a change in value at all is because of the change in demand for the stock. If the demand is high, the price will go up, but if the demand is dropping, it means public interest is declining. Thus, when asking the question of how much return you should expect on a stock investment, the answer will depend largely on what the public wants.

This same basic concept also applies in other investment forms. Whether you plan to invest in real estate, a retirement account, or some other instrument, you need to learn what causes the price fluctuations so you can gauge the movement of the market.

Ideally, you want to keep pace with these market movements. Whether your investment is in stocks, real estate, mutual funds, or something else, you need to be realistic in your expectations. If you're chasing after a figure like 12%, you're going to be disappointed. Knowing how the market works is merely the first step in creating a workable investment plan.

One way to boost your investment potential is to take advantage of compounding interest rates. For every percentage point increase in profit each year, you can earn massive boosts in your overall financial portfolio. As an example of this, consider the following point. Let's say you invested $10,000 at 10% interest and held it in place for your family to use in the future. After 100 years, it would have built up to more than $130 million. However, if you could somehow garner 20% interest on the same money, you would do far more than double your results. In fact, you would have accumulated over $800 billion dollars in the same amount of time.

Of course, holding an investment in place for a hundred years is not the goal of most people, but the illustration is clear. A good return is an excellent option, but if you can find investment tools that offer compounded interest, your returns will be thousands of times higher over time.

So what exactly should be considered a good rate of return? To determine this, you also have to allow for inflation. Your goal is to boost your purchasing power, but considering only an increase in dollar amount will not take a steadily rising inflation rate into consideration. In other words, you should not be looking for a specific dollar value, you should be looking at what you will be able to purchase with the amount of money you will eventually have. You want to know how many mortgage payments you can make, how many vacations you will be able to go on, or how many pairs of designer shoes you will be able to buy.

Basically, the true value of money declines over time. Hence, if you have $100 dollars today, you can purchase $100 worth of goods. However, that purchasing power would decrease over the years such that in ten years, you will be able to buy much less, and this trend will continue over time.

To see a perfect example, look at the Consumer Price Index published by the Bureau of Labor Statistics every month. They keep records that date back more than 100 years. The Index measures the changes in the prices of goods over time. If you study the charts, you will notice that the Consumer Price Index increased from a 1.0 in January of 2013 to 25.1 by November of 2017. This averages out to an increase of 3.1% per year. This does not mean that there was a consistent increase in prices for every year. A look at our history shows that during the Depression Era, there was a negative depreciation in prices that needed to be factored in as well.

As you start investing, you will notice these types of fluctuations that will continue to affect the results of your investments. You will notice periods where your earnings will come in fast and furious and periods where there will be little to no movement at all. However, if you do absolutely nothing with your money, it is a pretty good bet that every year, the money you are holding onto so fiercely will lose its value. Expect that your purchasing power will begin to decrease by approximately 3% with each passing year.

So, when creating your investment portfolio, your goal should be to increase your purchasing power by at least 3% every year to not lose the value you've worked so hard to attain. This is why investing is such an important strategy. While it may appear that saving money is a smart move, the minuscule interest rates that most banks offer are rarely enough to cover the rising cost of inflation that will eventually erode your future buying power. For that reason, the minimum rate of return you should expect from your investments should at least cover the inflation rate that we will all have to deal with.

How to Decide What Investment Opportunity Is Right for You

For anyone who is serious about getting ahead, the concept of investing should be clear. Still, this is just the first step in investing. Now, you have to decide which investment tool you will use and then learn the ins and outs of doing it.

If you've been thinking about this for some time, then you already know that there are more than a few options for you to invest in, each with its own level of risk and reward. Before you make the first step in investing, you need to do a little background research to get a good understanding of how each instrument works. You need to build up a basic understanding of what you can reasonably expect in returns and how you will manage the risks that are an inevitable part of this type of money-making strategy. You also need to know how it will gel with your investment goals and how it will fit in with other options that you will add to your investment portfolio.

Asset Classes

Generally, when investments are similar, they are separated into groups called asset classes. These are instruments that are similar in nature and offer the same type of returns and risks. There are several different types of asset classes, and within each class are several different types of investment options. Throughout the following pages of this book, we will look at several different asset classes that you might want to consider investing in; we'll take a closer look at each of the risks and possible returns along with some of the products associated with it.

There are quite a few asset classes you might consider, including investing in gold, real estate, stocks, bonds, and more. However, there is one asset that few people even think about when thinking of investment possibilities, and that's your own contribution to the investment portfolio.

Even before you decide to invest, you need to factor in the value of your skills, knowledge, and experience and how it will all fit into the picture. Your ability to earn money is crucial to your success when it comes to making an investment. Without money to start with, investment can never happen. Whether you decide to take a portion of your salary to invest or you decide to get the whole enchilada and start your own business, you will be banking on the value of your expertise in the global market.

Do not take this fact lightly. This will require you to make some adjustments to the way you are presently living now, especially if you are starting with a small sum of money. If you are living from paycheck to paycheck, you will have to start cutting back on your expenses. This may mean moving to a less expensive housing arrangement, cutting back on credit card debt, or putting in a bit more work to generate the money you plan to invest.

The younger you are, the higher the value of your human capital, simply because they don't usually have the cash to jump right into the fray. On the other hand, those who are in their forties or older do not have as much time to accumulate the returns you need. As you get older, the value of your human capital will begin to decline, you'll have fewer years to invest, and your ability to put in the extra effort to generate the funds to invest will also begin to wane.

You must make sure that the money you plan to earn on your investment will return results that will surpass inflation AND your spending habits. If it does not, then your investment strategy will not work, and you'll find yourself in a negative balance.

So how can you boost the value of your human capital when you're in your forties? You have two basic options. First, increase the amount of your earnings to compensate for any negatives. Second, decrease the amount of your spending.

Let's look at boosting your earnings first. Most people in their forties already have a stable job and a regular salary. However, it often does not keep up with their cost of living. You could go into your boss's office and ask for a raise, but chances are you won't get very far with that. However, there are other ways to boost your salary. You could consider offering your employer more services so he or she will be more inclined to increase your compensation. You might consider going back to school and getting additional education or training, or you could perfect your negotiation skills. At times, you may even have to consider pulling up stakes and looking for another employer that will offer you more. The key idea here is that you have to start with some type of capital so you can start building your investment portfolio.

Other people may be interested in starting their own business. This is not an option for the faint of heart. There are a lot of risks here, and it can be very difficult to get a new business off the ground. Even if you are successful, it may be some time before you can generate enough capital and afford to siphon off a little bit to start investing.

Once you have the capital you want to invest, it's time to turn your attention to the spending side. This is easier said than done. We are often inundated with things that marketers will insist we need, and you will have to make some painful decisions. Remember, the more you are able to cut back on your personal expenditures, the more you will have at your disposal.

Keep in mind that your human capital is always at risk and you need to think in terms of protecting it at all times. If you become ill or disabled, making sure that you have health and life insurance to protect you and your family from the loss is one of the first and most important investment decisions you can make. What happens if you pass away and you left no means of helping your family to carry on without you? This fact becomes even more important when you are an entrepreneur supporting a family. The very fact that your earnings are inconsistent at best is enough to serve as a reminder that you are always in a precarious state.

Return Risk Ratio

One of the things that often frighten people away from investing is the risk. They worked hard for their money, yet if they make a bad decision, all their work will go up in smoke. While there is a modicum of truth to that thinking, it is very one-sided. In our modern economic times, everything we trust is at risk. How often have you heard or even experienced people dedicating years of their lives to a job only to be laid-off, forced into early retirement, or—dare I say it—fired without warning? All the work and effort you put into it has just gone up in smoke, and you have little to nothing to show for it.

This problem is more prevalent than you might imagine, and it is especially disconcerting when you reach middle ages. The opportunities for older people in the workforce are quickly diminishing, and the idea of starting all over again from the ground floor is more than a little frightening.

The fact is, everything in life carries some level of risk. The question you must answer is how much of that risk you are willing to take. As they say, if there is no pain, there will be no gain. Investing, like everything else, comes with its own set of risks, so it's up to you to weigh each opportunity to determine if the risks are worth the potential gains you hope to achieve. There are no guarantees, so your ability to fully grasp the relationship that exists between the risks you are about to take and the possible rewards is a key piece of the investment puzzle. It will help you determine which investment route you'll be willing to take.

When it comes to investing, the general rule of thumb is the higher the risk you take, the higher the potential for a good return. For example, investing in cryptocurrency carries a high potential for return, but it holds an even greater potential for you to lose everything you put into it. Thus, you need to determine exactly how comfortable you are with your investment choices. You need to measure your risk/reward ratio.

One of the first questions you will need to ask is "can you lose money?" It's completely understandable for this to be one of your primary concerns. No one wants to lose money. However, there are other risks you need to evaluate as well:

- Will you earn enough to achieve your goals?
- If earnings are achieved, are you willing to up the stakes to boost your earnings?
- Are the investments you choose going to lose their value over time?

You can probably come up with a lot more questions when it comes to risks. The point is, these concerns need to be evaluated carefully before you make a decision.

One of the biggest worries any investor has is whether or not their investment instrument will lose value, taking all of their money with it. There are some places where you can put your money that can guarantee that you won't lose any value, but these usually come at a cost. Bank savings accounts, for example, will guarantee that the money you deposit will be protected no matter what happens to the bank. However, the risk here is that your returns are often very small, and placing your money with them removes it from other opportunities that could yield you a higher result. When you take the time to factor in the rate of inflation, most accounts will show that you are losing money over the long term. This is a kind of risk that few people are aware of. While they are getting the same amount of money back after years of depositing in the bank, they are actually losing their purchasing power. Ask yourself if this is the kind of risk you are willing to take.

You also need to consider whether or not the returns you are getting are enough to help you reach your financial goals. This risk is a little harder to measure. You will have to evaluate a number of other contributing factors to determine if your investment options are sufficient.

First, if you determine that you cannot afford a high level of risk, you may find that you have to put more of your capital into the investment to achieve the results you want. You will need to know just how much to invest to give you a better chance of attaining your goals. While a smaller investment will earn you more money, it may not be enough to help you achieve your goals.

Ideally, in these types of situations, the more time you have to invest, the better your chances. You also have to factor in additional expenses that you may not have considered. If you're investing in Certificates of Deposit in your bank, you may have to pay monthly maintenance fees, there may be taxes attached to your earnings, or there might be the almighty god of inflation that will want a cut.

The best way to circumvent these kinds of risks, which can erode the earnings you accumulate, is to make sure that your investments are diversified. When your portfolio is spread out and invested in a variety of things, you can lower your risk. While one investment may prove profitable at one time, it may be enough to compensate for any decline in other investment opportunities, thus balancing the scales and giving you another level of protection from total losses.

Chapter 2: How to Use Your Net Worth to Build Wealth

With each passing year, it is becoming more and more difficult to break even. Most of us feel like we're working harder and still falling behind. If you're not over your head in debt, you may still feel like you're running as fast as you can just to stay where you are.

This is where smart investment decisions can be instrumental in changing your circumstances. The problem is not in how hard you work, nor does it lie in the strategies you choose to use. In fact, it is more likely that you do not have a clear understanding of your personal financial situation.

In general, people tend to have two different mindsets when it comes to money. There are those who live from paycheck to paycheck and those who know and understand their true net worth. The person who relies on his paycheck is focused on building up his income to increase his wealth. Meanwhile, the person with an understanding of his net worth is focused on letting his money do the work for him.

This concept sounds pretty simple. As we learned in the last chapter, nothing happens until you invest in yourself, but it is what you do with that investment that will make the difference in how successful you'll be in your endeavors. If you don't yet recognize the difference, think of it this way. The difference between the two mindsets is the fundamental difference between income and wealth. On the surface, they may seem like the same thing, but there are some pretty significant differences between them.

From the moment we begin to understand the world around us, society has worked hard to get us to focus on money. They tell us that those who are wealthy have accumulated their wealth from working and earning huge six- and seven-figure incomes. Our parents tell us to get a job and work hard to get rewarded with more and more money. We learn to view our friends, coworkers, acquaintances, and everyone else we come in contact with by the size of their paycheck. In fact, our salaries and titles become status symbols for the rest of the world.

While income and wealth are certainly related, it helps to understand what they really mean. If you were to win the lottery and be awarded millions of dollars, the difference will become very clear very quickly. If you decided to splurge and spend it all in one year, you would probably end up with a fancy house, a luxury car, and all the amenities that go with them. You would give the *appearance* of wealth, but since you have done nothing to add to your net worth, it would be no different from the day before you received that big fat paycheck.

However, those who choose to concentrate on their net worth will fare much better for much longer. The key here is not how much you work or how much you earn—it all comes down to what you have and how much of it you can keep and build on.

This point bears repeating. It's not how much you have but how much you can hold onto that will determine your net worth and ensure your financial success. Your goal in investing should therefore not be to make more money but to make sure that you keep more of it. You want the money to reach a point where it can support you and provide you the financial security you need for you and your family.

As you can probably see, the paycheck mindset is very fragile and can break at any moment. You may think that your jobs and, therefore, your income is secure, but it will take only one financial faux pas for you to lose your job and that steady flow of cash will stop coming in. Getting laid off or fired from a job is a common occurrence these days, and if you're not focused on your net worth when that money source dries up, so would your security.

A person focused on his net worth will be much more stable when there is an economic downturn. It means that your resources and your source of financial support go well beyond a regular paycheck. If one investment option fails, you have others to fall back on, giving you the ability and the means to recover when you need to. In the end, rather than getting by, you'll actually have a tidy little nest egg to fall back in when crisis comes.

This is because as your wealth grows, your money will be working even when you are not. With the paycheck mentality, to get more cash flow, you will either have to work more, or you'll have to boost the value of your contribution to your employer to increase your assets. At a certain point, that will become impossible for everyone on this planet. If you invest wisely, there will come a point in time when you will no longer have to contribute to your investment pool because the money it will generate will start growing on its own, with little or no contribution from you. When that happens, you will no longer need to contribute more of the human capital you've been giving, and when the time comes, and you are no longer able to contribute, your money will still be coming in.

Net Worth

So how do you calculate your actual net worth and get this whole thing started? Calculating your net worth is pretty basic. You simply add the value of all your assets and subtract all the money you owe. What remains is your net worth. If you have a negative balance, meaning you owe more than you have, then you will have to take a few steps before you can begin investing in earnest. This may mean paying off some debt or cutting back on your spending habits.

Calculating the value of your assets can often be a challenge. Our homes, vehicles, jewelry, and other objects of value can also be added to the overall total of your net worth, and we tend to value their worth higher than others might. However, since they are not in liquid form, they are considered unrealized assets. In other words, you won't be able to take advantage of their value until you are willing to part with them.

If this seems like too much work, there are resources you can utilize to help you. Apps like the one found at Mint.com can do all the work of calculating for you. All you have to do is input the specific information, and you're good to go.

Once your net worth is determined, it is easy to see just how much money you have to invest. A general rule of thumb is to never invest more than you are prepared to lose, but you won't even be able to do that until you are aware of what funds you have to spare.

There are several ways to increase your net worth. You can start by setting aside more money, boosting your regular income, or paying down debt. Most people don't realize that cutting back on spending is one of the most basic parts of increasing net worth. Cutting back on the number of times you eat out or making one less trip to the shopping mall each month can make a huge difference in the value of your net worth over time.

You could also start by setting a significant long-term goal, but make sure that you create a bunch of smaller micro-goals to help you to achieve it. If you decide you want to have at least a million dollars before you retire, it may seem like an insurmountable task, but if you set that along with a smaller goal of earning $1000 the first year, $5000 the next, and $10,000 after that, and if you take advantage of those investment opportunities that allow you to compound your investment over time, it will seem much more doable and you will be less likely to give up before you get started.

The first micro-step you need to take is to create for yourself an emergency fund. This is where you set aside money for unexpected expenditures. This way, you will be less likely to take on more debt if an unexpected event arises. If your car breaks down, for instance, you would borrow the repair money from your emergency fund rather than using a credit card. In fact, some financial experts suggest that you set up an emergency fund even before you begin to pay your debt.

Even if you are living on a limited income, you can still do this. It may mean that you have to sell a few of your possessions or cut back on trips to your favorite fast food place, but these kinds of sacrifices show that you are working to build your net worth and not focusing on a set dollar value. Ideally, you want to put aside around three to six months of living expenses in your emergency fund so you'll have something to fall back on in case something unforeseen happens.

With all that done, it's time to start making some serious investment decisions. With a lower amount of debt, your net worth looks a whole lot more appealing. Here is where increasing your net worth gets exciting. To begin with, never take the short-term view on investing. Those whose sole purpose is to get rich quick usually make hasty decisions and end up losing a lot more than they bargained for. But well-planned and researched investment decisions made consistently over the long term can yield some pretty impressive returns.

Index Funds

One investment option that is a great starting point for the small-time investor is index funds. These financial instruments have been a very effective tool for the beginning investor. In fact, they have become so popular that more than 20% of every invested dollar in the country has found its way into index funds.

To fully comprehend what an index fund is, you need to first understand what an index is: a compilation of rules created to outline how to build an individual investment portfolio. Certain stocks and bonds that meet a given criteria are selected and added to the index.

For example, you may not realize that the Dow Jones Industrial Average is an index fund. It is a collection of thirty blue-chip stocks that are considered to be essential to the health of the nation's economy. Any stocks that are included in the DJIA are chosen by a committee of editors of the *Wall Street Journal*.

Another index you have probably heard of is the Standard and Poor's 500. These are the perfect instruments for first-time investors because you do not have to research each stock to determine its potential for making you money. These indexes offer you a host of benefits, including paying fewer fees and paying less in taxes. You can easily compound the tax savings and maintain them in your own 401(k) or IRA. These make a great first step in the world of investment and can yield pretty significant returns if you choose to hold them for the long haul.

Cash

After index funds, there are myriads of other investment options to consider. We'll discuss some of them briefly, starting with the easiest ones, and in later chapters, we will discuss many of them in more detail. Let's start with cash.

Most people do not think of cash as an investment tool, but for the new investor, it is the easiest. Everyone knows what it is and everyone wants it. Generally, if this is your first foray into the world of investments, it is likely the only asset you have in your portfolio.

Cash assets can come in more than just dollars and coins. It can also come in the form of bank notes, bank accounts, and money market accounts. Investments involving cash are often low-risk and are the preferred option for those with a fixed income.

Of course, the downside of cash investments is that you have no cushion to protect you in times of inflation, and the returns are not significant enough to maintain your purchasing power. Taking that into consideration, the negatives of cash investments may outweigh many of the positives. However, all of us need to have some cash stashed away in a savings account as these are the most liquid. In an emergency, you can gain access to the cash without much hassle.

Generally, a savings account will pay a higher interest rate than a checking account. However, the bank may impose certain restrictions on your money. You may be limited in how much you can withdraw and how often. If you're using a timed savings account, you may even have to pay penalties if you opt for an early withdrawal in case of an emergency. This is usually the case with *certificates of deposit (CD)*. This is a type of savings account where the money is deposited for a predetermined period of time (1-5 years). These usually pay a higher interest rate, but you will pay a hefty price if you want to withdraw before the appointed time.

With cash investments, you also need to keep in mind that while they are insured with the Federal Deposit Insurance Corporation, it does not mean that the total amount of your deposits is insured. Each account is covered up to a maximum of $250,000. If you choose these investment instruments, it is recommended that you not put more than that amount into any account. If the bank fails, becomes insolvent, or faces any other negative drawbacks, you will lose any money invested over that amount. Once your assets grow to more than that amount, you will want to move the excess into another account, preferably at another institution, to make sure you are protected.

Should You Hire a Financial Advisor?

There is no question that first-time investing is scary. The more you learn about what can happen with your investment dollars, the more you realize what you do not know. First-time investors are often not comfortable with trusting their instincts. They may feel that the risk is too high and want to hire a financial advisor.

But others may wonder if it is a wise decision. After all, financial advisors generally charge anywhere from a half to a full percentage of the total value of your portfolio every year. This could amount to a significant percentage of your returns. Are they really worth the money?

Of course, this is a personal decision that you will have to make. However, according to some reports, using a financial adviser can give you a significant increase in the returns of your investment. With the aid of a financial advisor, you could see as much as a 3% bump in your earnings each year.

However, not everyone is comfortable putting their assets in the hands of a stranger. Estimates show that only about one-fourth of investors feel confident enough to self-direct their investment portfolio. These are people who genuinely enjoy the investment game. They religiously follow the markets and enjoy making financial projections. They are also extremely disciplined and won't allow their emotions to take over and interfere with their well-thought-out investment strategies.

That leaves three-fourths or 75% of investors who are new to the game and may not be strong-willed enough to manage their portfolio on their own. While you may not be interested in an advisor who could help guide you to the best options, few people realize that they can still be of help to new investors by taking on the role of an investment coach. As you learn the ropes, a financial advisor can be a great shoulder to lean on, teaching you how to keep your fears and emotions at bay and showing you how to do the necessary research you need to make the right decisions.

The decision will depend largely on several factors. First, can you afford to pay the fee for them to manage your portfolio? And second, can you trust your own skills as you venture into this unfamiliar territory? Keep in mind that new investors often make decisions hastily—vacating a good investment right before it takes off, not knowing how to time the markets properly. The help of a good financial advisor could be instrumental in helping you avoid the common pitfalls often experienced by these novices.

How to Deal with Risk

Let's face it. You're entering an arena where risk is a big player. Whether you choose to invest in stocks, bonds, mutual funds, real estate, or precious metals, there is always the chance that your money will lose its value. There is even the chance that it could go totally bust. The fact is, there is no investor that has never lost something on an investment decision, but that does not mean that your investment plan is doomed to failure.

First, you have to really come to grips with risk. When you make an investment, you are deciding what to do with your assets, but you are never sure of what the actual outcome will be. All the numbers may be pointing to a positive return, but anything can happen, and everything could easily go bust.

Some point out that investing is risky because the prices are not consistent. Prices fluctuate up and down on a daily basis, and the more volatile and risky the investment tool, the more the price will fluctuate. A drop in price does not mean that your decision is bad, though. It could be caused by the current market conditions or the result of a management decision to expand the business, to incur more debt, or to merge with another company. It could also be the result of government decisions if you're investing in an opportunity in another country.

Simply put, risk is the possibility that you will have a negative outcome that can affect your investment dollars. The goal is not to eliminate risk—to do that, you would have to have control over everything associated with your investment, which is literally impossible— rather, it is to minimize that risk to a level you can live with.

To do this, there are several things to keep in mind. First, know your risk/reward ratio before you begin. Reward is just the opposite of risk: it is the possibility that there will be a positive outcome for your investment. Let's take the stock market, for example. Historically speaking, the risks are higher when you invest for the short term. Those who choose to invest in stocks for the long-term generally receive a higher average on their annual returns than those who focus on short pops in price (around 10%). Second are those who invest in corporate bonds (6% average), Treasury bonds (5.5%), and Treasury bills (3.5%).

Of course, these are all industry averages and do not present any specific guarantee, but they do show an indication of what types of investments have less risk and how much time you might have to wait to see positive returns.

While these averages can help you to decide if you're willing to take the risk, it is not always easy to know what to do. Even strong and historically profitable options can take a plunge without warning. You also need to carefully consider the timing of your investment and the fees that may be associated with it. Remember the basic rule of investing—buy low and sell high. This means that you should not just wake up one day, drop your money in the pot, and wait for a return. This type of impulsive decision almost always ends in lower returns. Buying when the commodity is hot and when there is a lot of interest will surely push the price up. You may learn that you're buying at a point when the price is about to peak, which will raise your risk. If that happens, you may have to wait a long time for the price to recover, if it ever does. It is possible that the price will never return to that point again and you would have lost a significant part of your money.

There is a delicate art to timing markets. You have to walk a fine line between deciding whether to ride out the ups and downs over the long term or to jump in and out with each price movement. Life is unpredictable, and you need to be prepared for such volatility before you start. While you can never completely eliminate the risk, there are some things you can do to manage it:

1. *Asset Allocation.* Make sure that your investment portfolio has a collection of assets that will spread your risk over several different industries. By including different types of assets in your investment (real estate, bonds, stocks, etc.), you lower your chances of one industry falling short of your expectations and taking all your money with it. Never put all your eggs in one basket.

2. *Diversify.* Even within a particular asset class, do not put all your money into one form. For example, if you are investing in real estate, avoid putting all your money into housing. Consider investing in REITs or in rental property, vacation rentals, etc. By spreading your investments across a variety of areas, you ensure that at least some of your choices will prove profitable.

    You might also consider investing in another type of asset to offset the losses you accrue from another investment. This can provide insurance and give you an additional means of managing your risk. The bottom line: there are no guarantees when it comes to investing, but by better understanding how to reduce your exposure to risk, you can enter the market with your eyes open and make smarter decisions that have a better potential of boosting your earnings.

Dealing with Reality

Investing for newbies can be quite scary. You work hard for your money, and it may feel counterproductive to expose it to risk. However, we've already learned that it is going to be at risk whether you invest it or not. This is the reality of life, and you need to be prepared. One of the most effective ways to understand this is to remove emotion from the equation.

If you decide to invest in the stock market, for example, you will see the price of your stock rise and fall like a yo-yo. Your natural impulse will be to pull out almost as soon as you dip your toe in the water. However, you need to take a more practical and productive approach to your investment decisions. You need to have a more realistic view of the markets. It is uncanny how new investors jump into an investment at its highest price and sell at the lowest. This is because they often fall for the media hype or they get caught up in the FOMO fever—the Fear of Missing Out. This type of emotional investing can be avoided by keeping just a few simple basic concepts in mind.

As you've probably already gathered, timing is crucial when it comes to investing. There is often a lag period between the time when a related event is reported in the media and when the actual event occurred. Keep in mind that the media reports events only after they have happened. Unless it is expected to be extended, your investment is likely already in recovery phase by the time you hear the news. Thus, there is no need to have a knee-jerk reaction when you hear negative reports.

Consider using dollar-cost averaging. This strategy allows you to invest equal sums at regular intervals. It is an effective investment approach in all market conditions as the amount of your investment is averaged out over the life of the investment. So, when the prices are high, you will buy less; when the prices are low, you buy more. You will take advantage of the downtrends by purchasing more, and you will be able to reap higher returns when the prices go up again.

At the same time, when the prices are up, any portion of your investment you purchased during a downtrend is producing higher capital gains, and while you're still purchasing at the higher price, you are only purchasing a few while gaining the rewards at the lower prices. The secret to success with dollar-cost averaging is to stay the course regardless of what happens. The more you get involved with the ins and outs of the market, the more you put your money at risk.

It is not always easy to take the emotion out of investing, especially because of your attachment to your money. However, history shows that the more emotion you apply to your investment plan, the more mistakes you are likely to make and the more losses you can occur. The volatility and the multiple factors that can impact any market can be frightening, but remember, the more you take the time to understand, the less emotional you will be about it.

By taking a realistic approach, your investment strategies take on the shape of paying your bills. It is simply a part of real life, and if you can separate those inner feelings from your decisions, you'll have a much better chance of success.

DOWNLOAD YOUR FREE BONUS:

77 Wealth Secrets

Go to: http://bit.ly/wealthsecrets77

Chapter 3: A Word About Insurance

It can be difficult to understand why you need to pay for insurance. For some people, it could appear like you're just giving your money away, but the reality is that insurance is a very necessary part of investing. While months or even years may go by without anything happening, buying insurance is an investment in the most important asset you have: yourself.

You may have worked hard to build up a nice financial position as a means of protecting your assets, and it makes sense that you will want to protect it. Accidents and disasters are not planned events and can happen at any time. If you are not properly insured, it could mean that you lose everything you have worked years to build, leaving you in financial ruin.

By the time you've reached your forties, you will likely have already built up a pretty good body of assets that you want to protect. It is strange how most people will fight to the death if a burglar were to break into their home and try to walk away with even one of their prized possessions, but when it comes to protecting it from disasters and unexpected events, they seem to be at a loss.

You can be confident that you can insure just about anything you own, but there are a few fundamentals that no one should live without.

Types of Insurance Everyone Needs

Insurance that everyone should make sure to invest in include life, health, and property insurance. These are the bare minimum when it comes to protecting your assets.

Life Insurance

Most people already understand the importance of having life insurance. When you're young, you often feel like this is an investment to put off until later, and while you are less likely to worry about dropping dead from heart attacks and strokes, even the youth of our modern world can find the end approaching much faster than they have imagined. But when you're in your forties, this investment is even more important.

There are many different factors to consider when trying to decide how much life insurance you need. If you already have life insurance, that's good, but you need to also consider if you can find the same coverage at a lower price. Remember, wealth starts with how much money you can hold onto, not how much you make. If you've had your policy for a while, you might also want to consider if your lifestyle has changed—it may need adjusting. Perhaps you want to add another beneficiary or change the one you have.

Other factors that could impact your life insurance include the following:

- The results of a medical exam
- The details of your waiting period
- The type of life insurance you have (term, whole life, or permanent life)

There are some policies that have an investment option attached to it. For the new investor, getting a policy that invests a portion of your premium could be a fast and easy way to make money.

Health Insurance

Of all the insurance policies you might need, health insurance is likely the one that makes most people cringe. It is not cheap, and it can be easy to reason your way out of having it. Not only do they have expensive monthly costs, but you may also have to come up with a considerable copayment when you need medical help.

For this reason, many people decide that they don't need health insurance. They reason that if they are healthy, they cannot justify the extra expense; they figure that if a medical issue does arise, they will simply pay for it when it happens. However, this could be a huge mistake, especially for those who are entering middle age.

Medical treatments are costly, and an unexpected health issue could literally leave you bankrupt. It only takes one medical emergency to bury you under a mountain of debt with no foreseeable way out. This usually happens because of the exorbitant medical costs, but it is also compounded by the fact that you have just lost your human capital: incapacitated, you'll be out of work. You not only have to deal with recovery of your health and the costs associated with it, you'll most likely not be in a position to generate income for an extended period of time.

In addition, health insurance comes with a legal aspect to it. It is now mandatory under the Affordable Care Act, so you will likely also be faced with fines if you don't have it. The bottom line? Health insurance is not an option. To protect your most valuable asset, it is a must to ensure that all the work you put into generating the income and capital you plan to invest will not be lost due to one small slip on your part.

Property Insurance

Finally, you need to consider getting some property insurance. Your investments can come in many forms. Putting money aside to make large purchases like a home or an automobile are probably some of the largest expenditures most people will undertake. Yet, these things are always at risk in some form or fashion.

Having good property, automobile, or some other form of insurance is essential. When we are young, we do not usually possess such large and costly assets, but as we mature, we begin to see the lasting value in these things. One incident could literally wipe out years of hard work and commitment it took to acquire them.

As you begin to think deeper about investing, your mind would likely drift off to things like stocks, bonds, currencies, and such. While these are important aspects of your investment portfolio, it is best to consider these options *after* you have secured protection for the assets you have already acquired. Your goal is to hold onto as much money as you can, so you don't want to run the risk of losing any of it because you failed to protect what you already had.

It is not enough to have insurance; you should review your policies regularly, making absolutely sure that you have adequate coverage for everything. If you add on to your home, always make sure your homeowner's policy is also updated. If you add a new driver to your household, make sure that it is included in your insurance coverage. By doing all of these things, you have put yourself in the investor's mindset, and you're ready to take the next step into investing.

How to Use Insurance to Build Wealth

Few people really understand how having insurance can work wonders in helping you to build wealth. As a matter of fact, some advisors refer to it as the "most holy" of accounts. So let's take a look at how insurance can help you to retain as much as 40% of your income for the long term. There are several very good reasons why you might want to consider building your wealth in this way:

1. Any money you put into your life insurance policy does not have to enter the tax system again. Therefore, you can avoid paying a considerable amount of taxes.
2. With the right policy, you are less likely to suffer any losses over the long term.
3. When your money is stored in a policy, it is more liquid. That means you could easily have access to at least 70% of your funds at any given point in time, without any fear of exposure to taxes, penalties for early withdrawal, or fees.

There are several things to consider when you are trying to build wealth using insurance. First, you need to do research to you make sure that you are choosing the right company to buy your insurance from. Take the time to review everything available to you. The company you decide to work with should demonstrate financial strength, a solid history, regular dividend payouts, etc.

Ideally, you want to look for a company that is mutual. That means the primary ownership is in the hands of the policyholders, not the shareholders. This is important as it gives you the ability to participate in the profits of the company by means of a dividend payment. You will want to look for a company that has high financial ratings and excellent consumer reports.

The company must have a significant history behind it. A study of its history should show if it is consistent in its business dealings. The companies that meet all of these criteria are on a pretty short list with a track record that spans a hundred years or more.

Second, you want to examine the policy. You are looking for a Whole Life Insurance policy. This allows you to accumulate dividends, and it also gives you a guarantee that your premiums will not increase over time—a plan where you can invest as much as is legally permissible to be paid into the policy.

Get a term insurance rider. By adding this to your policy, you can artificially inflate the face value of the policy so you can contribute more without any fear of tax issues later on. It will give you a faster means of accumulating your returns so you can reap the benefits without fear of reprisals.

It is important that you save as much as you possibly can. Follow the 40% rule. Based on past statistics, the top 1% of the world's wealthy saved as much as 40% of their income before taxes. If you can use this as your benchmark, great, but if that much isn't possible for you, no worries. Try to invest at least 10% and build on it as time passes.

Of course, this decision is not entirely up to you. The insurance company will have to examine your finances, and they will determine the maximum amount you will be allowed to contribute. Once they determine your maximum, you can decide how much you can afford to put into this type of investment.

Investing in insurance can get complicated, so it's important that you get the right insurance representative to work with. Ideally, you want someone who can work within your goals and expectations. If they can't get behind your expectations, then you'll find yourself working with someone whose only interest is to sell you more insurance.

Believe it or not, there is a lot of money to be had in insurance. It is an easy, low-risk investment option, but you still must be careful to choose a company and an agent who is willing to work with you to create a workable plan, allowing you to invest in a way that will help you accumulate wealth in the remaining years you have to work with.

DOWNLOAD YOUR FREE BONUS:

77 Wealth Secrets

Go to: http://bit.ly/wealthsecrets77

Chapter 4: Learning About Equities

One of the first things to learn about investments is that there are myriads of ways to help your money grow. Chances are, you've heard quite a few different terms discussed over the media as well as around the office where you work. You may know that they are investment tools, but you might not be sure exactly what they are.

Equities is one of those investment options that have many people confused. Investing in equities is pretty much the same as investing in stocks. You are actually purchasing a small share of a company and, as a result, you are also entitled to a share of the profits, which may be paid back to you in the form of dividends or in the form of a repurchase wherein the company buys back its own shares from you. The company has the option to reinvest their profits back into the business rather than buy back its shares or pay out a dividend. In that case, you would earn your profits through an increase in the value of your shares.

Some may wonder, "Why invest in equities?" They perform in exactly the same way as a stock, so where do the differences lie and what significance do they have? Actually, there is no real difference between a stock and an equity in terms of performance. However, with stocks, investors are allowed to purchase an equity interest in a company so that they can share in the profits. The company benefits because it is a means of raising capital without going into debt.

Equity, on the other hand, has a much broader concept. When you own equity shares, it generally refers to owning the actual value in a particular asset or business. You can own equity in a business, in real estate, or in the form of stocks.
Simply put, stock investing is just one type of equity you can own. In basic terms, equity can be used to refer to the combined value of the equity and liabilities, which make up the total value of the assets.

There are several ways you can analyze equity returns to determine if it is a good investment. The most common method is to look at an equity index, which is a collection of individual company stocks. You've probably already heard of some of the most popular indices. The Standard and Poor's 500 is a list of 500 of the largest companies in the country. It is weighted based on each company's market capitalization, so the larger the company, the larger its weight will show on the index.

There is also a daily index return that allows you to evaluate the performance of an index on a single day. These calculations are determined based on the results of each individual stock listed. This type of return can include calculations with or without dividends. If dividends are excluded from the calculations, it is referred to as a price return; if included, it is called a gross return or a net return. Ideally, you want to look at the price return as it shows what returns you will receive from owning that particular equity.

If you analyze the returns on the S&P 500 over the historical period between 1957 and 2017, you will notice that the return on investment was around 10.2%. The nation's rate of inflation over the same period was approximately 3.7% per year. This is a good indication of a profitable index.

You also want to look at your possible exposure to risk. Usually, this is determined by the volatility of price ranges, either daily, weekly, or monthly. Study the volatility (or the rate of price movements) over each period to see how much fluctuation it may have.

Another measure to carefully study is the maximum drawdown, which measures results based on the buys and sells at the worst possible point. For example, suppose an investor were to purchase an equity just moments before a financial crisis and then sold it at its lowest point. Looking at its history, showing these worst possible scenarios will provide a pattern that indicates which periods were ideal for investments and which returns were not. You can gauge this type of result over long- or short-term periods and use it to determine the best points to enter or to exit the market.

Of all the equity indices to choose from, the S&P 500 is the oldest and the most recognized, but it is not the only one—there are hundreds of indices to choose from. You can find them based on geography, sector, and even classification. Each index has two primary functions: 1) they provide a clearly defined and easily understood way to build wealth and 2) they function as a benchmark for a number of active investment products.

Geographical Indices include only those companies that are located within a single country or region. In the beginning, you may only be interested in those companies that are found in your own locality. While this type of location bias is quite normal, as you get your feet wet in the investment game, you'll eventually want to protect your investment by diversifying and branching out into other areas as well. Historically, it has shown that when the economy in one area begins to falter, other areas are getting stronger. By diversifying and spreading your investment dollars to other regions, you capitalize on this natural phenomenon.

Sector indices are those equities that are grouped by a specific sector or industry. There are some sectors that have a very small maximum drawdown. These are considered defensive sectors, so they are less likely to lose value when the market corrects.

Style indices are those equities that are classified based on the scope of the index.

These could be based on a company's market capitalization. They could be large-cap, mid-cap, or small-cap indices. You might also find growth indices, which lists those companies that are showing a much faster growth rate than other, more commonly known companies.

Other style indices could include how a company is weighted in the index or other factors. The point here is that there are hundreds of indices to choose from, and you can purchase an equity based on the very parameters you set for yourself. In fact, new equity indices are entering the market at an extremely rapid rate, so what may not be available for you today may surprisingly be available to you tomorrow.

Investment Products

A recurring theme in all investment circles is to diversify. There are many ways you can diversify your investment products to maximize your potential returns and lower your level of risk. When you are investing in equities, there are three different investment methods you can try.

1. Active investment
2. Passive investment
3. Direct investment

Which method you choose will be based on the type of index that is most likely to give you your expected return. You could also factor in the amount of time and effort you are willing to commit to your investment strategy.

An active equity fund collects money from individual investors and invests it on their behalf. As an investor, you would subscribe to the fund and collect your returns when you exit. These are usually run by fund managers who are responsible for making all the decisions on behalf of their clients. You will usually have to pay an investor fee that goes to the manager of the fund. You will also have to pay a performance fee, which is based on any funds that go above the expected benchmark. Other fees may also be associated with investing in this type of fund.

With such fees associated, you want to make sure that your returns will be enough to cover them when you exit the fund. You can invest in this type of equity through your bank's online banking system or by starting a monthly investment plan with scheduled periodic investments automatically paid into the fund.

Passive equities work similar to the active indices, but they track their returns differently. Active equities are attempting to outperform the historic indices, whereas passive funds are trying to get as close to their performance as possible. There are also costs associated with these indices, but they tend to be considerably lower than active funds.

These funds do not require a sophisticated team of managers, only a simple administrator or custodian to monitor the fund. There is a management fee that is given to the fund manager, and there may or may not be additional fees for subscriptions and/or redemptions. Make sure you choose a fund that has the least expenses. Passive indexes usually have a minimum investment amount which could prove to be quite significant, so if you plan on investing a small amount, it may be smart to choose another option until you have raised more capital.

Exchange Traded Funds

Exchange Traded Funds (ETFs) are simply another type of passive index. The fund invests in the companies that are defined by the specific index. The difference between ETFs and mutual funds is that ETFs do not have subscriptions or redemptions. Instead, the investor buys or sells the ETF on the stock exchange. In such cases, you will have a commission and be paying a bid-ask spread instead. While your goals remain the same, you want to minimize your expenses: with ETFs, the cost of trading needs to be factored into the equation as part of the expenses.

These instruments have three different methods of replication:

1) Full replication where the ETF has a 1:1 investment in the companies on the index.

2) Optimized replication where the ETF may not invest in every company listed in the index (or not with the same weight).
3) Synthetic replication where the ETF is not actually investing in the index itself. It may instead contract with a financial institution to handle the investment portion.

Of the three different options, many advisors believe that synthetic ETFs should be avoided because there are additional risks associated with the investment bank. If, for some reason, the bank defaults, it can be very difficult to track what happens to the money. Investors stand to lose a significant percentage of their investment dollars if that happens.

Direct Investment

Many individual investors have opted for the direct investment approach. This is usually done through a stockbroker rather than with a fund manager. In such cases, you make all the decisions on which stocks to buy and sell yourself. By doing this, you save on management and performance fees and can even eliminate the need to pay for a custodian to oversee the activity of the fund.

On the surface, this seems like a no-brainer. You would definitely save on all the fees and other expenses associated with an ETF but, unless you have significant experience and knowledge about these types of investments, your chances of matching or outperforming the indices could be very slim.

An additional problem would be the amount of capital you would have to put up. With a broker, the investment capital could be very minimal, but as an individual investor, these would be treated separately and could be considerably higher. To get the most out of each trade, you would have to pay a much higher fee and make larger trades.

Managing your own investments may seem exciting and fun, but you will have to invest a great deal of time and effort to be successful. For new investors, lessons are most often learned through trial and error, which can turn out to be quite costly. You will have to have faith in your own skills and the emotional discipline to stick to your plans even when things do not turn out the way you expected.

Understanding Currency

When trading equities, you'll find that many of them give you the option to trade in different currencies. The two most common currencies are the US dollar and the Euro. Many equities can be found trading on several different exchanges and currencies, and it is possible to find them with varying expense ratios.

If you find the ETF you're interested in is trading on several different platforms, there are a couple of things you need to think about. You could opt to buy in the dominant currency—dollars or Euros, for example. If you do choose to invest using a different currency, you should do all your research based on the charts for that currency as the performances will be different. If not, expect that you won't be able to get reliable results when you measure the overall performance of your investment.

Another point to consider is hedging. Currency hedging is a means of protecting your investment against the volatility that often exists in currency exchange rates. There are several different types of equity products that are used as currency hedges. This is an excellent option for those who are limited to a fixed income. Keep in mind, though, that currency hedging is not always the best option as the volatility that already exists in equity trade is usually greater than the volatility that is common in the foreign exchange markets. You have to weigh the costs of this type of hedging to make sure that you're not paying more and getting less for your efforts.

How to Time the Market

Once you have decided which ETF you want to invest in, there is one more crucial element you must apply before entering the market. Because this type of market shows incredible volatility, it is best to know when to get in and when to get out.

There are obvious benefits to knowing how to time the market well. A perfectly timed investment can help you avoid the negative periods when the stock prices plunge and take advantage of those periods when there is a marked increase, and you can reap some pretty impressive returns.

But there is much more involved than getting in and out of the market at the right time. To capitalize on your profits, you need a strategy that will help you identify the periodic upturns so you can reenter the market at a lower price and start the cycle over again.

Make sure to factor in all the costs attached each time you enter and exit the market. You need to feel confident that you will gain enough of an uptick to earn you a tidy profit and cover those additional fees as well. Otherwise, you'll end up losing money.

This can be tricky as many reports show that individual investors often lose money simply because of poor market timing. While there may be many reasons why this is the case, the general consensus is that human beings tend to put emotions and psychological factors in play when making decisions. This leads us to the most important question: Is there a proven system that can improve your chances of timing the market more accurately?

There answer is yes. There are several systems that will work in some situations—but not in others. It is best to test various systems to determine which ones work for your particular portfolio. Each system has its own set of parameters that may apply to different factors, so what may work for one person may not be the system that works best for you. As you invest more and more into the market, you may also find that a system that worked best for you in the past will suddenly no longer work; you'll have to change your strategy to keep your investment returns coming your way.

One strategy that has been very effective in avoiding market timing errors is to completely disregard it. Rather than trying the hit-and-miss approach, many opt to use dollar-cost averaging, a method where you decide to invest a set dollar amount at a predetermined time period on a regular basis. These investments could be weekly, monthly, annually, or at any other time interval.

Because the market fluctuates up or down frequently, you average your investment payments over a longer period of time. This way, while you do not get the all-time lows that may be reached, you're not saddled with the all-time highs either. When the price goes up, the overall value of your investments also goes up; when the price goes down, the overall value of the investments can also drop. The good news is that the losses are not as pronounced as they would be if you invested a large sum of money at the wrong time. Then, you would be forced to wait a long time for the price to recover before you can cut your losses.

Exiting the market is a lot simpler. If you are a long-time investor, the decision to sell can easily be timed by watching the market. Ideally, you want the investment to continue to compound over the years and only deduct the money when you absolutely need it. Even then, determine to only take out exactly what you need so the money remaining can still work in your favor.

DOWNLOAD YOUR FREE BONUS:

77 Wealth Secrets

Go to: http://bit.ly/wealthsecrets77

Chapter 5: When You Have a Fixed Income

As we get older, everything in our lives tends to start settling down. Many end up living on a fixed income with little to no leeway one way or another for investing. It can be a challenge to find a few extra dollars to squeeze out safely without losing out on something else you depend on. But that does not mean that investing is completely out of the picture.

When you are living on a fixed income, you need to make your money grow more than ever. Some people who are on disability or have a very set salary with no wiggle room will have to look at certain investment tools that can help them grow their income without putting too much stress on their current financial situation. Following are a few options to consider when you are living on a tight budget.

Short-term Bonds

You might want to start your portfolio with a selection of short-term bonds, which pay higher interest rates than money market funds or certificates of deposit. What makes these investment options so appealing is that they lose very little principal compared to other longer-term bonds if the interest rates start to rise.

To buy short-term bonds, you need to do a little research first. You can start by looking for the prices and the yields at TreasuryDirect.gov government bonds. For corporate or municipal bonds, you may have to go to an investment broker to get the information you need.

The market prices should already include the markup for the dealer's profit, but you need to make sure that they have an investment grade rating for an independent organization like Moody's or Standard and Poor's 500.

Fixed Annuities

Fixed annuities usually come with a guaranteed minimum return that can range anywhere from 2.5 to 3.5%. Your investment is protected against loss—something that is very important for those living on a fixed income. Any income you earn is tax-deferred, making them much more valuable. Another advantage of fixed annuities is that they typically won't lose any principal even if the interest rates start to climb.

Another reason why annuities are so popular is that investors always know exactly how much they're going to get in return. If you're looking to get a steady return on your investment, that is exactly what you will get.

There are a few steps you should take before buying an annuity:

1. Do your research. You want to look for those that have high financial strength ratings. Technically, buying an annuity is like buying a promise to guarantee income. Make sure you select one through an insurance company that has the ability to stand behind that promise.
2. Look for several different annuities; don't put all your money into just one. Diversify.
3. Annuities are not guaranteed by the FDIC and are instead guaranteed by your state's insurance guarantee system. Know the maximum they will guarantee and don't invest any more than that.
4. Make your investment gradually, not all at once. The size of your payout will depend on several factors, but it's best to buy in stages. This will protect you from any risk of buying into an annuity when the interest rates are too low. When the rates go up, you can add more.

Dividend Paying Corporations

If you want to dip your hand into the stock market, look for corporations that are willing to pay dividends. Look for those businesses that have a consistent history of giving increases over the years. You can find a list of hundreds of such companies at Dividend.com.

Companies with a long history are ones that are least likely to go bankrupt one day, taking all your money with them. You can find dividend-paying stocks that are as low as a few dollars to hundreds of dollars a share. Depending on your budget, you can buy them at will, and if you reinvest your dividends when they are paid, you could easily see a nice and hefty return with each payment.

You can buy dividend-paying stocks through a broker, but if you're on a fixed or limited income, you could avoid paying the commissions and fees by buying through sites like Robinhood.com or FolioFirst.com. These sites do not have a minimum purchase, so if you want to start off by buying one single share of a stock, you can. As the dividends build up, you can use your dividends to purchase more. In the beginning, it may be slower to build your wealth, but in time, the investment will start increasing all on its own.

When you are living with a fixed income, it can be difficult to find an investment tool that gives you a safe but profitable place to put your money. But that does not mean that there are no investment possibilities out there for you. In fact, you'll find that in this day and age, getting into a profitable investment possibility is fairly easy to do.

Active vs. Passive Fixed Incomes

You can also boost your income by investing in fixed-income funds. Your goal with these funds should be to build it up to the point where the returns can match or even surpass your current income status. You can accomplish this by investing in a specific selection of securities that will provide a consistent and steady return. These can be invested on a subscription basis where you make regular payments into the fund, allowing the returns to compound over the years until you reach your set income goal.

Like all other investments, you will have to pay fees, but if you choose wisely, they will only be a small percentage of your overall return. An annual management fee may cost you 1% of the value of the portfolio, and there will probably be a subscription fee which could amount to a fraction of a percent. Another .5% will be paid when you are ready to redeem your investment.

These are very easy investment instruments to get started with. You can find out more about the different active funds by looking at the S&P Dow Jones "SPIVA US Scorecard." You will find a detailed analysis of these types of funds in 13 different categories: government, corporate, and municipal bonds are just a few.

Passive funds can also be very low cost and often turn out even better returns than active funds. You can find them the same way you find ETFs. Vanguard maintains a long list of these funds, many with a long history of very low-cost investments. You could invest in a single passive income fund that invests in the government's total fixed-income market with a low expense ratio of .06%.

Crowdlending

One final way for those with a limited fixed income to invest is through crowdlending. In our modern world, we see new platforms appear that are open to new small-time investors. Crowdlending is a way to become your own bank; you can loan money directly to another individual or small business. The general concept is that you can give a partial loan to borrowers and build up a very broad portfolio in the process. Sometimes referred to as peer-to-peer lending (P2P), it is an easy way to generate income quickly.

One of the best things about crowdlending is that it can be done at an amazingly low cost. You are working exclusively through the Internet. These companies are not saddled with expensive overhead costs like banks and other brick-and-mortar institutions. In some cases, you may find that you can participate in a program without incurring any fees at all. Currently, traditional lending investment opportunities are not offering ideal yields on an investment, which makes participating in crowdlending extremely attractive.

There are already dozens of crowdlending platforms established. If you Google them, you'll have more than your share of options. However, not all of them are reputable, nor are they all going to work in your best interest. Many of them are just starting and are therefore not in a position to be analyzed or judged as being good or bad. Others are so new, they have little to no chance of surviving the next financial crisis. However, below is a list of some of the most profitable platforms for you to consider.

The Lending Club (https://www.lendingclub.com/)

This is the largest crowdlending platform in the world. You can open an account with as little as $1000 to get started.

- Loans are given to individuals and small businesses
- Each borrower is graded from A to G with A being the highest grade and G being the riskiest
- The borrower pays both principal and interest monthly
- The loans are not guaranteed, so if the borrower defaults, you could lose your investment
- There is no collateral to cover your losses
- The platform will attempt to collect but may not be successful (collections may incur additional costs)
- There is a 1% fee that a borrower pays to its investors
- You have the option to wait until the entire loan is paid in full before you receive your return or you can sell the loan to another investor and collect the rewards immediately
- Average returns are somewhere between 4.3 and 6.5% per year before taxes

Mintos (https://www.mintos.com/en/)

This is a European-based platform that has seen some pretty positive results over the past decade. It was founded in 2015 and is based in Latvia. If you are interested in crowdlending in foreign currencies, this may be a good option.

Assetz Capital (https://www.assetzcapital.co.uk/)

Based in the UK, Assetz Capital allows private investors to lend to small businesses and developers. Founded in 2013, it is currently looking for new financing from investors both inside and outside the UK.

At this point, you should be able to see that even those who do not have a significant amount of cash to invest can start to see their money working for them. Just like with all other investment types, you want to always keep your portfolio diverse so that you can protect yourself against losses and lower your chances of risk.

Chapter 6: Investing in Real Estate

Almost everyone on the planet understands the value of having real estate. Even those who are not seeking to grow their wealth recognize that real estate is good to have in anyone's portfolio. At the very least, owning your own home is an important symbol of success. However, for the investor who is looking to build his wealth, the possibilities are immense.

There are several different types of real estate depending on how deeply you want to be involved in your investment. For example, you may start off with residential real estate by purchasing your own home and then expand into apartment rentals, single-family house rentals, commercial real estate, shopping malls, restaurants, vacation properties, offices, factories, warehouses, farmland—the list goes on. And just as there are many different types of real estate, there are also numerous ways to invest. The most obvious is to buy property outright, a practice that dates back thousands of years.

Historically, residential real estate has seen a price increase of approximately 3.2% per year since records started being kept in 1890. This is an extremely important figure to remember as it allows the appreciation of a home to keep up with the average rate of inflation year after year. Even if you do not earn a profit, you will still maintain your purchasing power.

Of course, there will always be occasional downturns, but historically, the ability for real estate to stay ahead of the curve is one of the reasons it is the most popular form of investment. This does not mean there is no risk at all. During the Depression and in more recent years, the real estate industry has struggled to stay above water. This is mainly due to the fact that the vast majority of real estate investments require financing, and buyers can quickly find themselves in a precarious position for a number of different reasons.

Still, by and large, investing in real estate is still the most well-received form of investment to date.

Residential

While the primary goal of any real estate investment is to see the value of the property increase over time, it is not the only benefit you receive from owning your own home. You save in a number of ways, including the money you can keep from not having to pay rent every month.

When you purchase a home, it is usually done with a combination of your own cash in the form of a down payment, and the balance paid off through a mortgage, which can be amortized over many years. This means that you will pay a portion of the mortgage each month along with a percentage of interest.

Some would like to equate a mortgage payment to a rental payment, but it is not exactly the same. When you rent your home, the money you pay is gone forever, but when you pay a mortgage, the principal amount paid simply moves from your cash stores and becomes equity in your home. With each payment, you own a little bit more of your home than you did before and the bank will own a little bit less. In the end, you are free to sell it for the best price you can get and keep all of that cash for yourself. In essence, you are paying yourself each time you make a mortgage payment on your home.

Whether you own a rental home or an apartment, you can expect to have maintenance costs. If you share ownership of a building, these expenses will be shared with other owners, but whatever the case, you need to factor in these costs to the amount of rent you charge.

You also need to be concerned with renovation expenses. These are often in addition to regular maintenance costs, which generally go to the regular upkeep of the building. For example, sewage fees can be considered regular maintenance, but renovations that involve replacing pipes several times during the life of the building are not. These expenses can be hefty so you may need to finance these or take out credit with your local financial institution.

The best way to handle these additional expenses is to plan ahead for them. By setting aside a percentage of the rent to manage renovations, you can be confident that you will have the funds on hand when they are needed and avoid the need to go into debt to pay for them.

If you plan to own the property for a long time, understand that there will come a time when you will need to replace the floors, kitchen, and bathroom; repaint; rewire, and replumb. By planning for these things long before they become necessary, you can not only save a lot of money but also keep the value of the building from declining.

Unexpected events can also happen, so you need to make room for insurance coverage in your rent as well. Floods and fire are common occurrences that can happen in every area. Having a policy that protects you from these types of damages is essential if you're planning on using your property as rental income. The cost of insurance is minuscule in comparison to what you would lose without it.

Other things to factor in when investing in rental property are taxes and other incidentals. Before you decide to invest in these types of properties, it is essential that you lay out the plan carefully and make sure that the rents you charge are sufficient enough to cover all these expenses, including occasional vacancies that occur between renters and still give you a nice profit in the end.

You may think that the additional costs of upkeep and management are high when you own rental real estate, but compared to the amount of money a renter pays for the same property with no lasting benefit, the answer is clear. After putting pen to paper, you'll find that owning rental property even in the bad times can be very profitable in the long run. But to make that happen, it is crucial to follow a few basic guidelines when you're searching for the right property to invest in:

- Pay the right price. Make sure that you are getting a competitive price for the property and that it is not overpriced, making it difficult for you to earn a profit. The price should be based on the location—properties located within the city or by the sea often demand a higher price than those in remote areas or the suburbs. The size of the property can also affect the price, along with the view, number of rooms, and condition.

- Make sure you calculate your potential returns carefully. Getting a good price on your property is not a guarantee that you are getting a good deal. You will need to get a realistic view of the community where the property is located and the average cost of rents for comparable properties and compare that with what you will have to pay in mortgage, management, maintenance, and taxes. It is best to be conservative in your estimates so as not to be met with any nasty surprises later on.

- Look for properties that are in demand in the community.

Once you've decided on the property you want, it is important that you manage your mortgage risk. Mortgages can be either variable or fixed. A variable mortgage means that the interest rate is a general level plus the spread. For example, you could get a 12-month interest rate plus 1%. If it is a fixed mortgage, it will stay the same with no change throughout the life of your mortgage.

Fixed interest rates are usually higher than a variable rate, and you will more than likely pay more than with a variable. However, you will know exactly how much you will pay each month. You won't have to worry about incurring additional costs associated with your loan over the years, and there will be no additional risk.

Which loan you decide on will depend on your personal circumstances and your preference. There is no right or wrong way to finance property. Study all the options and decide which one works best for you. Ideally, you want to make sure you're in a position where you won't be forced to sell because of some unforeseen circumstances that may occur, which, considering the length of your loan, is highly probable.

Vacation Properties

Another real estate investment few people think about is vacation property. There are many pros and cons in relation to this type of investment, so it is not a good option for everyone. When you purchase a vacation property, you invest your equity in the property and then finance the rest. You benefit as the owner of the property by taking your rate of return and deducting the costs of maintaining the property and dividing the result by the equity you used when making the purchase.

There are a lot of hidden costs associated with vacation properties. In addition to the cost of the property itself, there are legal fees, utility charges, registration costs, and maintenance and service fees. To make a profit, you must be sure that the fee you charge your vacation renters is enough to cover all these fees and leave you with a tidy profit.

When you own a vacation property, you may have to pay community fees (depending on the location) and renovation costs and factor in building depreciation (if you own an older building). Management fees, taxes, utilities, insurance, and maybe even accounting fees are also considerations.

If you don't plan to be on site, you will need to hire a manager to take care of all of these hidden expenses and make sure that your tenants have a good experience during their stay. Many of these managers could charge as much as 15-20% of the total amount of rents collected. While that may seem like a large sum, if you account for all of that in your vacation rental fees, you will be more than covered.

Keep in mind that if you decide to purchase a vacation property, you will be forever connected to the community it is located in. It is not always easy to know what to expect in the future; all sorts of things that could turn potential guests away could happen, leaving you with a hefty expense to deal with. The reality is that bad things do happen, and you will need to be prepared for it. Make sure that an occasional rental over the years will pay for all contingencies down the line.

REITs

REITs or Real Estate Investment Trusts are probably the easiest way to invest in real estate. These trusts are actually companies that own real estate and lease them out to a particular sector. You might have a REIT that leases only to medical facilities and another one that leases to shopping malls.

While there are many positives associated with REITs, there are definitely some disadvantages you need to be aware of. There are often some very high costs associated with maintaining these types of public properties. For one, the vast majority of income received will go to pay for the salaries and overhead costs of maintaining them. In addition, because they are equities, their results generally follow the same trends as the equity markets so their returns can be quite volatile. As a matter of fact, during the last financial crisis in the USA, REITs saw a near 80% drop in profitability for the duration.

You can find REITs on many of the equity market indices. They are publicly traded companies, so if you are already invested in low-cost, passive equity funds, there is a good chance that you are already invested in REITs.

If you have decided that you need more real estate in your portfolio, REITs is an easy way to get that done. You won't have to take out an expensive mortgage, nor will you have to worry about pesky management details. REITs are traded in the same place you would buy stocks and bonds. There are two different Vanguard ETFs where you can invest in real estate not just locally but around the world.

Look for REITs through any stock brokerage company, and you will find many. However, there are other REITs that are only available through brokers and financial intermediaries. These more private REITs are not always the best options. The brokers charge astronomical fees, the REITs often have poor performance, and they do not always deliver on their promises.

It is very important that you use extreme care and only purchase REITs that have been proven to be reputable. Some private REITs had been found to be Ponzi schemes, so use extreme caution. If you buy them through a broker or a public exchange, you should have no problem.

In addition to the profits you can gain from the rising value of a REIT, many of them pay a monthly dividend. If you are looking for a regular income to keep you afloat, allocating a portion of your portfolio to REITs is a great way to do it.

DOWNLOAD YOUR FREE BONUS:

77 Wealth Secrets

Go to: http://bit.ly/wealthsecrets77

Chapter 7: Investing in Commodities

Another highly profitable asset class is commodities. These can be divided based on different categories. Some of the most common commodities you may be familiar with are oil or natural gas and agricultural commodities like soybeans, milk, coffee, and sugar. Livestock commodities include hogs and cattle, and metal commodities include natural elements like gold, copper, or silver. To find commodities to invest in, look at the commodity index. The S&P 500 GSCI Commodity Index is one of the oldest listings of commodities in our history.

There has been a regular record of commodity performance going back to the 1970s showing that the average annual return on investment is around 3.1%, which is quite competitive with the rate of inflation for the same time period.

Before you decide to invest in commodities, you need to understand and respect your risk tolerance. Suffice it to say that commodities can be a highly risky investment and there is no shortage of investors that have lost more than half of their money in a very short period of time because of it.

To invest in a commodity, you don't have to purchase the commodity directly. You can invest in a related company that is active in investing in it themselves. When the price of the commodity increases to a point higher than the cost of production, the company profits—and so do you. You can also choose to invest in low-cost ETFs as another option.

There are two basic arguments in favor of investing in commodities. First, they make a good hedge against inflation, and second, the returns are not based on the stock market returns. If you are planning to invest in the short term, both of these arguments should be important to you.

If you have a relatively high-risk tolerance, investing in commodities could be a very good option for you. While the risk of losing could be quite high, those that pay off in the long term are often immensely profitable.

Gold

Gold has been around for thousands of years. It precedes paper and coin currency, which have often lost their value through inflation or from governmental conquest. We all understand inflation and how it can erode the value of any asset we own, but the effects of governmental conquest are not always clear. Imagine that you were a citizen of one country where the currency was strong and carried a great deal of weight. If that country were to be conquered by another, how much value would your paper currency have? Chances are practically zero, but if your assets were in the form of gold, it would be accepted in any country around the world without question.

This shows the lasting power of gold. It is the one commodity that is expected to retain its value regardless of the economic climate. If you were to look back at gold's price history, you would see that it has seen an increase in value of 7.3% per year on average for the last 40 years. With inflation fluctuating between 3 and 4% per year, you would have netted yourself a tiny bit of profit if you had invested in gold during that time period.

These are impressive numbers, but there have been quite a few influences that have made that possible. First, prior to 1971, the US government had issued a Gold Standard which had kept the price of gold stable for decades. When that standard was eased, the price of gold could rise as high as the demand for it. So, for the next decade or so, the price of gold saw an increase of at least 16 times. After that, the price leveled off to about 1.6% per annum, but for the same time period, inflation seemed to remain at a steady increase. Hence, if you had invested in gold in 1971 and held it for those four decades, you would have seen a healthy return. But if you had invested in 1980, you would have probably lost a good chunk of your money waiting for gold to reclaim its former glory.

This just shows that investing in commodities can be unpredictable at best. Timing the market and paying very close attention to current events that could affect the price is crucial to protecting your investment. Gold has limited uses in today's market (used as jewelry or in the electronics industry), and it has no cash flow. Thus, most of its value stems from the fact that it is considered in most societies as another form of physical cash that is limited in supply. Bear in mind that you also run the risk that it would no longer be accepted as a form of money one day and will, therefore, lose its value.

You can see why the glitter of gold is precarious at best, but if you choose to make this type of investment, there are several ways to purchase it. Contrary to the way most forms of currencies are viewed, it is still highly unlikely that gold will lose its value any time in the near future—at least not before other forms of currency fail. It is believed that if we ever meet another time of high inflation in our future, gold will outlast them all. It is more likely that paper currency will lose its value long before gold does.

If you're the kind of person who wants to be prepared for the worst, gold may be the investment option for you. At the very least, it could be beneficial to have at least some of your portfolio invested in gold. There are several ways to do this.

First, you can buy shares in a gold-producing company. If you already own diversified equity funds, you likely already own a percentage of one of these companies. The difficulty with this strategy is that these companies may not be able to provide you with the kind of diversity you need. As publicly traded companies, they are expected to follow the same trends as the other equity markets; if there is a crisis, gold may not be as liquid as you need it to be.

Another investment option would be to by an ETF that holds physical gold. The gold in these funds are kept in vaults and are provided in different denominations. To find out more about these ETFs, here are a few places you can visit:

1. iShares Gold Trust
2. iShares Physical Gold ETC
3. UBS ETF–Gold

There are other ETFs that do not hold physical gold, but they do purchase gold derivatives from investment banks, which in turn will provide the ETFs with gold returns.

You can purchase gold bars and coins directly from gold dealers. However, you need to be very careful if you decide to do this. Not all dealers are reputable. You may have heard of the Gold American Eagle coin, the Canadian Maple Leaf, and the South African Krugerrand. These are highly rare gold coins that are valued more as collector's items rather than as a store of true commercial value. The price of these coins may not follow the standard gold price, and they may be hard to sell if you ever need to cash them in. Dealers may not always represent the true gold content of these coins either. Without a reliable test to verify the amount of gold in each coin, you may find yourself paying for more than you're really getting. If you choose to purchase gold through a dealer, make sure you go to a reputable dealer that has an established reputation for honest trading.

When buying physical gold, there is also the issue of storage. It is not recommended that you keep it at home. Instead, keep it in a vault at either your financial institution or another place that can secure its safety. Here, you are not only concerned with its actual theft but also with a recorded chain of possession. All of this will incur fees that could easily strip the value of the investment right out of your hands.

However, if you time the market correctly, it is possible to make a pretty nice sum in the precious metals markets. Whether you are purchasing gold or silver or any other type of commodity, you need to exercise extreme care and be very diligent in watching the market. These instruments can be very volatile, and you could lose it all in a matter of days or weeks. On the other hand, if you have the stomach for it, you could conceivably catch a huge windfall that could give you very promising returns in a very short period of time.

Investing in commodities has not always been an attractive option for building your wealth, but if you are already committed to a broad commodity equity index, chances are you already own some form in your portfolio. Gold, silver, and other precious metals, however, work very differently from other commodities so they should be considered to be in an entirely separate class. Since it is extremely difficult to predict how precious metals will move, most people purchase it as a form of insurance against extreme economic declines. While it has the ability to outlast most paper currencies during such negative times, in normal periods, it is likely to underperform. At best, invest in small sums of precious metals, but keep the bulk of your investment dollars in other areas that may prove to be more profitable.

DOWNLOAD YOUR FREE BONUS:

77 Wealth Secrets

Go to: http://bit.ly/wealthsecrets77

Chapter 8: Cryptocurrencies

Before the fall of 2017, cryptocurrency wasn't even a consideration for most people, but when the price of Bitcoin—the first of more than a thousand of these digital currencies—saw a hike to nearly $20,000 for one, heads started to turn. There is no doubt that the returns seen in the cryptocurrency market are eye-popping, to say the least. They definitely eclipse the kinds of returns seen by other investments by far. But is investing in cryptocurrency the right choice for you? There are a few things you need to know about this market that can help you to decide.

Usually, by the time you reach your forties, you have a lot more on your mind besides building wealth. You need to be very concerned with protecting your assets so that you'll have something to live off of in your later years, something to pass on to your family and others you care about, and something to help your children get their start in life. The volatility of cryptocurrency could play a significant role in those kinds of decisions. It alone is probably the main reason why many financial advisors do not recommend it is a viable asset for building wealth. However, a closer look at the possibilities may reveal some incredible merits to the crypto world.

The entire crypto market saw an exponential growth in market capitalization from $17.7 billion to over $800 billion in a single year.

That's more than 4500%, a feat that no other investment market has ever accomplished.

Cryptocurrencies are not the first digital currency introduced to the world. We've been dealing with digital currencies ever since modern technology introduced online shopping, online banking, and direct deposits of our paychecks. What makes cryptocurrencies stand out is their blockchain technology and its ability to disrupt the financial position of a wide number of industries.

With blockchain technology, users have a decentralized database that is highly transparent and inherently secure, devoid of many of the flaws and weaknesses of centralized platforms. The concept is quite revolutionary and is the primary reason why so many people are attracted to it. With decentralization comes empowerment wherein control of their money is placed back in the hands of the people and not in a third party.

Up until recently, many people have viewed cryptocurrency with suspicion, a sort of gamble, so to speak. Some even called it a pyramid scam wherein those at the top reap the rewards and later investors skim off all the profits and leave the others with nothing. The extreme fluctuation of the market is also well-known. When the market reached its peak in January of 2018, there was excitement everywhere, but a few weeks later, when the market began its correction with a sharp drop in the value of all crypto, those cries of excitement turned into anguished laments. Still, many people still view cryptocurrency as a great investment opportunity that is easy to get into and gives impressive rewards.

Cryptocurrency Risk/Reward Ratio

The key to success in investing in cryptocurrency is to have a thick skin and an ability to manage risks carefully. In fact, according to some analysts, your ability to monitor the markets and actively manage risks properly will account for at least half of the returns you will receive.

Because of its newness in relation to other investment instruments, cryptocurrencies do not have any specific rules, patterns, or guidelines you can follow. It has been described by some as the "Wild Wild West of investments." You will have to follow your instincts when it comes to this market, and your chances of gains are about the same as your chances of losses.

A word of warning is warranted here. One thing that almost always destroys any profits gained in the cryptocurrency arena is greed. It can be thrilling to see when your coin is increasing in value, and the natural tendency is to stay in the game and ride the wave all the way to the top. But remember that in this world, things can change suddenly and without warning. Avoid being sucked in by the media hype when the coins are on the rise. They can make you believe that some coins are completely unstoppable, but there is always going to be a point where the rise will come to an end. There will always be a correction, and a crash is inevitable.

If you decide to trade in cryptocurrency, set your target dollar amount and vacate the trade when you reach it. It doesn't matter if the price continues to rise afterward; it is the eventual crash that you want to avoid. If you're still keen on riding the wave, you can always get back in after you have realized your profits.

Find an Exchange

There are myriads of ways you can invest in cryptocurrencies, but before you can buy even one coin, you will have to get set up. One of the first things you'll need to do is buy a cryptocurrency wallet. You will be trading in digital money, so there are no physical coins to hold on to. All cryptocurrency needs to be stored in digital form.

There are several different types of wallets to choose from, including the Paper Wallet, which is simply a physical record of the keys that give you access to your money. Each time you want to transfer or withdraw your cryptocurrency, you will do so with encrypted keys. Without the keys, even you won't be able to access your money. The purpose of the wallet is to have a secure place to store your keys, keeping your investment secure.

Once you have your wallet, you need to open an account with a cryptocurrency exchange. These work in a similar fashion to the stock exchange; it is where you can purchase cryptocurrency. When your account is active, you can begin purchasing cryptocurrency in any amount. Even if you don't have enough money to buy a whole coin, each coin is divided into 100,000,000 smaller amounts (called satoshis for Bitcoin). So, if you want to buy Bitcoin, and the current price is $10,000, you can purchase a percentage of Bitcoin in satoshis. If you use dollar-cost averaging, you can eventually accumulate enough satoshis to make up one whole Bitcoin.

For new investors, starting with an easy exchange is often best. Many go to Coinbase: it is the easiest exchange for newcomers. But Coinbase is limited in terms of coins to choose from, offering only Bitcoin, Ethereum, Ethereum Classic, Litecoin, and Bitcoin Cash. However, this is not a problem as you will need to purchase other alt-coins with these coins given that most other exchanges will not accept US dollars. Once you have an account set up on Coinbase, you can then transfer your coins to other exchanges to purchase other coins you may be interested in.

All cryptocurrencies are not available on all exchanges, so if you plan on investing in different coins, expect to have accounts with several different exchanges like Binance, Bittrex, BitMex, BitFinex, Poloniex, Kraken, and Coinmama.

Strategies for Investing in Crypto

Once you have coins, you will have to develop a trading strategy. Many people prefer to trade where they get in and out of the market in a short period of time while others prefer to invest their money and wait for the coin to increase in value. Depending on the health of the market, this could take anywhere from a few days to a few years; you will have to exercise patience. Whatever option you choose, here are a few fundamental guidelines that will help you get the most out of your investment:

- *Sell when the price is on the rise*: Always try to sell when the price of the coin is going up. It may be tempting to try to reach the top, but that could be a good way to get caught in a trap. Anticipate a price and sell before it peaks. This way, you can get out of the market before the mass flood of sellers comes in. Some analysts recommend doing it when the price has tripled in value. That will allow you to get your seed money out, and it will still leave you with double the profits. Some investors never sell all of their assets, leaving a small percentage in place to continue to grow with the market.

- *Diversify*: This has been stressed over and over again in the book, and diversification is also extremely important when it comes to cryptocurrency. It is essential to an effective risk management. Try not to invest more than 30% of your crypto money in a single coin. A simple guideline would be something like this:
  - 30% Bitcoin
  - 20% Ethereum
  - 20% Litecoin
  - 20% other alt-coins
  - 10% ICOs
- *Split and reinvest profits*: To compound your reward after you have collected your profits, split it and reinvest. You can decide for yourself how you want to split the profits, but here is a suggested formula to get you started:
  - 30% can be reinvested in alt-coins
  - 25% can be reinvested in Bitcoin
  - 25% can be reinvested in ICOs
  - 20% can be drawn down into US Dollars

By following these basic rules and guidelines, there's a good chance you can turn a profit investing in cryptocurrency. However, keep in mind that this is probably one of the riskiest investment strategies there is. You may make a return in a few days, weeks, or months, but it could also take years. As a general rule of thumb, never invest more in cryptocurrency than what you can afford to lose. That way, when one of your coins does make a run, the rewards will be that much sweeter.

ICOs

ICOs or Initial Coin Offerings should not be confused with purchasing an actual coin. ICOs are simply a means of raising funds for a coin they want to introduce to the world as the next digital currency. You could actually view an ICO as a crowdfunding event in which the first coins (tokens) are purchased in return for your investment dollars. It is very similar to the IPOs issued on the stock exchange, with the exception that you are purchasing tokens rather than actual shares. All cryptocurrencies start as ICOs and sell their tokens in exchange for seed money to get their new coin established.

Of all the cryptocurrencies available, investing in ICOs is the riskiest. These are coins that are not established; they have no track record and may not ever hit the market. However, if you pick the next winner, you might see a giant windfall similar to what happened with Ethereum, which raised a whopping $2 billion dollars in a matter of only nine months, giving a giant cash return to its initial investors.

If you're willing to take the risk on an ICO, here are some very basic guidelines you want to keep in mind:

- *Study the whitepaper carefully and evaluate the use cases*: You want to see

just how feasible the new coin is and determine if it has present or future value that will appeal to a large number of people.
- *Look for the project's minimum viable product readiness*: Look to see if the project is ready for market and what problems might be anticipated with its usefulness. Find out what problems it is expected to solve that may already exist.
- *Do a comparison check*: You need to know what kind of competition it is facing and what other products exist that are attempting to address the same problems. Look for the specific features this coin will use to address those problems.
- *Weigh both the negatives and positives*: You want to know everything—the good, the bad, and the ugly—about the coin and determine what kind of returns you might reasonably expect in the future.
- *Learn as much as you can about the team*: Every coin has a team of experts. Read their bios and see if they are adequately qualified to launch such a project. Make sure you have both a good product and a good team behind it. What experience are they bringing to the table? This will require studying the website and their social media profiles. Follow their announcements and launches and determine buyer sentiment in social media channels.

- *Study their roadmap*: Make sure the team is sticking to their plan and not deviating from their initial goals.
- *Find out how they will be using their funds*: As the money is collected, it should be clear how it will be utilized. Most ICOs will use the funds to build up their technology with some funds dedicated to research and development and cybersecurity. Alarm bells should be ringing if the lion's share of the money is going to marketing rather than development. While a percentage of the fund should reasonably be set aside for marketing, the most promising ICOs will focus on developing a good product first and focus on marketing more towards the end of the project when they are ready to officially launch.
- *How many coins will be in circulation*: Ideally, the better the future it has, the more tokens will be available for distribution. If the project is holding back the bulk of its coins, it is cause for caution. You need to know why they are not releasing more into the system.
- *Compare it to other successful coins*: This will help you see how close they are to an already proven system.

The odds of earning a lot with an ICO can vary depending on a wide range of circumstances. Those who do best are the ones who have done their due diligence and did the necessary homework to determine an ICOs future chances of success.

Top Earners

Cryptocurrency is now a billion-dollar industry. With the right conditions, it is possible to garner a tidy fortune overnight. This is a market that moves fast—decisions are made at the speed of light. Right now, there are more than 1500 cryptocoins on the market, with more being introduced every day. It is pretty clear that this is an industry that has a strong foothold and the potential is high.

Still, of those 1500 coins on the market, not all will make the grade. As an investor, it is up to you to decide which ones will push through the crowd and reach the top. If you're new to this industry, it is best to focus most of your energies on the top earners in the market. Only after gaining a bit of experience should you try your hand at some of the newer and lesser-known coins on the market. Below are the safest coins to invest in, the ones where you are less likely to lose a sizeable chunk of your money.

- Bitcoin
- Ethereum
- Litecoin
- ZCash
- Dash
- Ripple
- Monero
- EOS
- NEO

- Steem

It is a good bet that these are the coins with the longest-lasting staying power; however, nothing is guaranteed. As a new investor, only you can decide if you're willing to take the plunge with these or if you're brave enough to venture off the beaten path and try something new.

Is It Worth the Risk?

There is no doubt that investing in cryptocurrencies is risky. But for some, those risks are totally worth it. Here are a few things you should know before you make any decision:

1. Unlike other investment tools, cryptocurrencies do not have government backing, nor are they supported by a central bank.
2. If you choose to store your currency online, you would not have the same protection you have with your bank account. There is no federal insurance to protect your assets.
3. They are extremely volatile, and the value can change constantly, with prices ranging thousands of dollars within just a few hours or days.
4. There is no guarantee that it will ever recover if the price drops.

Remember to always do your research before making any decisions about investing in coins.

Look at its history, read claims from others, and determine for yourself if the promises are a scam or not. This is not a decision to be made hastily, but if you have the stomach for such a venture—*and* you choose correctly—the windfall could all be worth it.

DOWNLOAD YOUR FREE BONUS:

77 Wealth Secrets

Go to: http://bit.ly/wealthsecrets77

Chapter 9: Lesser-Known Investment Opportunities

Anyone who is new to investing could easily be overwhelmed by the sheer number of opportunities that exist today. With each new asset class, there are several different methods to turn a profit. We've all learned about the stock market, cryptocurrency, real estate, and a host of funds to choose from. These are the most common and easiest ways to start getting your money to work for you, but they are not the only ones.

The general idea behind investing is to put your money into something that will increase in value. For example, you may choose to purchase a vehicle and consider it an investment, but because the car will lose value during the time you own it, it is not really an investment regardless of its cost. However, you can make purchasing cars an investment depending on the type of car. Choosing to buy a vintage car or an antique would take the purchase to a whole new level.

With that concept in mind, look around you, and you will see hundreds of investment opportunities that you may not have considered before. Consider some of these investment options that many have made a profit on:

- Racehorses
- Sports teams

- Endangered properties
- Wine
- Art
- Collecting

The entire list could be quite extensive; the possibilities are endless, and the potential for great earnings could be very high. The key is to educate yourself as much as possible about these options and measure them against your own risk/reward ratio to determine if they are the right option for you.

Start-Up Business

We've already discussed the value of human capital. It is the only asset class you have that you can totally rely on. If you have a unique skill or talent that is marketable, starting your own business could prove to be very profitable.

When you have your own business, you are not working for a paycheck—you are laying a foundation on which you can capitalize on your talents and grow your wealth in the process. If you have a little capital saved up, there are a few things you need to keep in mind to lower your level of risk and gain the most from your investment.

1. **Own Your Name.** Whatever name you choose for your business, make sure that you trademark it AND your website's domain name. Check to see that the trademark is available by doing a

trademark search at the US Patent and Trademark Office website at http://tmsearch.uspto.gov/bin/gate.exe?f=tess&state=4805:rje7u7.1.1. By making sure your name is exclusive to you, you could literally save your business from a host of legal problems that could evolve down the line, especially once you've become successful.

2. **Make Sure You're Up on Legal Matters.** Become familiar with all the legal regulations and licenses you'll need to run your business. You can do the research yourself, but because many legalities are technical and detailed, it may be worth it to hire a lawyer to do this for you. This includes matters like tax laws, licenses, employee rights, and other regulations. Generally, these things do not become apparent until you have become successful: you could run your business for years, but once you reach a point where you're making a profit, all sorts of problems could come out of the woodwork with the potential of eating up all your profits, leaving you destitute.

3. **Budget Carefully.** Never invest all your money into a new venture. You have to be smart about how you use your available funds. Determine ahead of time how much money you need to live off of and make sure that those expenses are taken care of first. Investing in a business can be very exciting, and when

you get those dollar signs in your eyes, it can be difficult to see straight. By keeping your head and preparing for the chance that your decisions do not pay off right away, you can protect yourself from experiencing a loss that could cause you financial troubles in the future.
4. **Mentally Prepare.** Owning a business is just as much a mental game as a financial one. You will no doubt work longer hours than you would at a regular job, and you're most likely going to have to wait for several years before you see a significant payoff. Make sure that you are mentally and emotionally prepared for such a commitment and plan everything out carefully before you begin.

Investing in a new business is the same as investing in yourself, and it could be the smartest move you make. There are more than a few businesses that started with only a few hundred dollars and eventually grew into six or seven-figure businesses in a matter of years.

If possible, start small with a simple online website and grow from there. This allows you to launch with a minimal amount of money up front and expand as your business grows. Others start with a simple blog or as a consultant for other businesses. With the advances in modern technology, getting a new business started is easier now than it has ever been.

US Treasury Securities

If your investment tastes tend to be on the more conservative side, you can see your principal money protected from extreme market swings by investing in US Treasury Securities. These are basically obligations issued by the US Treasury Department used to fund the enormous national debt. You are basically lending the government money with each security you purchase. You can purchase them based on maturity dates that could range anywhere from 30 days to as long as 30 years.

To purchase these securities, you can visit their portal at https://www.treasurydirect.gov/indiv/products/products.htm. You'll find the securities in denominations as small as $100. When you are ready to sell, you can visit the same site.

DRIP

The term DRIP is an acronym for the Dividend Reinvestment Plan. By purchasing investment tools that pay dividends and then reinvesting those dividends back into the plan after they are paid, you can accumulate a vast amount of money to get started. Some stocks pay dividends bi-annually, others pay quarterly, and there are also quite a few that pay out monthly.

The best way to take advantage of DRIPs is by using the dollar-cost averaging strategy, which averages out the price at which you buy stocks. This way, you are never paying the highest price for a share nor are you paying the lowest.

This makes for a low-cost way to accumulate more shares of a company without having to shell out a lot of money in the process. You can invest in DRIPs directly through the company; many offer their shares at a discount for participating in their program. These programs also come with no trading commissions, making them even more appealing.

If you're not interested in buying directly from the company, you can also buy the shares directly from an exchange and reinvest the dividends on your own, but this will require you to have more hands-on activity in the investment process.

Money Market Accounts/Certificates of Deposits

Money market accounts generally have very low returns, but they are some of the safest investment instruments for the wary investor. There are several pros and cons to this type of investment. First, it is a great place to put in excess money you have around so that it can work to build your wealth. Especially considering how volatile other investment avenues may be, those with anxiety over investing will find money market accounts a great way to get their feet wet.

Liquidity is not an issue either. Because they are usually in very high demand, you will find you can buy and sell them at will with few problems. This means that you can jump in or out without any negative downside or loss of money.

However, the returns you get on this type of investment are not always stellar. It is possible that the value of the return would be very close to or even just below the inflation rate. If that happens, while you won't lose any principal in the investment, you could lose purchasing power on the money. If left in for an extended period of time, it is possible to lose a percentage of the overall value of the investment before you are ready to cash it in.

These also come with expenses. Even small annual fees can take a toll and eventually eat up any returns you have earned. Even though they are purchased at your local financial institution, it is possible that some of the money you invest in these funds are not protected by FDIC, which means that if something were to happen to your bank, you could lose it all.

Certificates of Deposits are also a good place to start investing. They are very low risk, and you can fully expect that on maturity, you will get the full value of your deposit back plus interest. Even if the institution you purchase them from falls apart, they are insured under the government's FDIC, so you have no fear of loss.

Motifs

Motif is a unique investment platform where you can contribute to an already existing mini-mutual fund created based on a very specific set of criteria. You might choose a motif based on solar energy, recycling, or some other cause you feel strongly about. There are hundreds of different motifs to choose from (you can research many of them here https://www.goodfinancialcents.com/motif-investing-review/).

There is a minimum investment of $250, but each motif could be a collection of up to 30 different securities. You will also have to pay a transaction fee to invest or even to create a new one. Before you choose a motif, you need to learn as much about them as possible. Some more common categories you can find include the following:

- Consumer products
- Industrial solutions
- Maritime exploration
- Medical applications
- Military & defense

Under each category, you will find a list of stocks that are included in the Motif, so you'll know exactly where your money is going and what percentage of it is supporting each stock.

FolioFirst, Robinhood

If you are interested in investing in the stock market and you don't have a huge enough sum of money to start, using sites like FolioFirst or Robinhood are great options. Both of these sites charge no commission, so all of the money you use goes directly to your purchase of stocks.

You will have to take some time to get set up, but once your account is approved, you can begin trading in earnest. You can contribute as little as a few dollars with each deposit, or you can set it up for automatic deposits to go directly to the account. So, rather than starting out with expensive broker commissions (some could be significant), you can start your investment plan with enough money to buy a low-cost stock and then build on it without having those extra additional fees.

Pros and Cons of Robinhood

Pros:

- Easy account setup (less than five minutes)
- Wide selection of stocks to choose from
- Fast and easy trades
- Accessible both online and through smartphone APPs

Cons:

- No DRIP program; dividend reinvesting must be done manually
- No fractional shares; every purchase must be a complete share
- No tools to analyze stocks
- No IRA, Roth IRA, or 401(k)

Pros and Cons of FolioFirst:

Pros:

- Allows purchase fractions of shares
- Offers monthly investment plans starting at $10
- Has ease of use

Cons:

- Limited stock selection
- No instant trades (actual price could vary because trades are not immediate)
- No DRIP program
- No IRA, Roth IRA, or 401(k)
- No tools to analyze stocks

Both of these companies are great starting places for new investors, especially if they're working with limited funds.

DOWNLOAD YOUR FREE BONUS:

77 Wealth Secrets

Go to: http://bit.ly/wealthsecrets77

Chapter 10: Pitfalls to Overcome

There are many reasons why people struggle with investing. Most of them are based on fear. While schools are very diligent at teaching children math and formulas, few ever dedicate any time to teaching students investment strategies. Hence, many people hesitate to get involved because they are unsure of what they are doing.

This is sad since investing can change their lives in so many ways. Investing doesn't have to be something you are afraid of, and it certainly doesn't warrant the extensive worry that has so many people sitting on the sidelines. Yes, it does take a little time to learn the ropes, but once you start, you'll find that it isn't as difficult as it may seem.

You will face some pitfalls and dangers that may cause you to hesitate, but there are ways to overcome those negative issues and help you launch a very effective investing campaign that could open the door to all sorts of possibilities.

Procrastination

Many put off investing either because they feel they just don't understand enough or they lack the interest to do the research. This is perfectly normal, but by the time you reach your forties, your mind begins to settle down, and your interest in the more adventurous activities that could keep you busy are slowly replaced by the weight of the responsibilities you've accumulated. Others may put off investing simply because they just don't have the time and energy to put into it.

Regardless of the reason, once you realize that investing doesn't have to be as difficult or time-consuming as you might think, it should be enough of an incentive to get you started. As you've already learned, there are hundreds of different investment opportunities. The hardest part is finding an investment avenue that will allow you to build your wealth without the need to consume too much of your time.

Even if you do not have a strong urge to invest, the benefits to be gained could be enough of an incentive to get you started. In reality, once the returns start flowing in, it can become addictive, and you may find that you want to keep it going no matter what.

Not Having a Plan

Another pitfall that may cause you to stumble as you start investing is not having a plan. Once you get started, you need to have a clear direction with specific targets and goals in mind. Having no plan at all could put you on the path to failure. Investing is a systematic approach to finances. Investing at regular intervals and knowing when to get in and out of a market are key strategies that can protect your interests. Without a plan, you may get in at the wrong time or exit an investment too soon.

Not having a plan also gives more room for panic when the market doesn't perform as expected. You need to develop a long-term plan showing what you expect to gain and set benchmarks to show your progress. By doing this, you know exactly where you are and where you are going, and you can easily figure out the steps you need to get there.

Setting Realistic Goals

Keep in mind that effective investors have goals. The more in advance your plan is, the easier it will be to achieve it. But it is not enough to know that you want an income of $100,000 a year by the time you retire. You need to have smaller goals that will stair-step you toward your progress. Starting to invest in your forties will inevitably put you ten to twenty years behind the starting gate, but that doesn't mean it will now be impossible to achieve your ultimate goal.

You need long-term plans, so you don't quit halfway to your mark, and those plans have to be attainable and realistic. When you have planned your increments correctly, you will have a repetitive step that is systematic and consistent. Know how to HODL or hold on for dear life when the investment is good and, when an investment is bad, know how to cut losses.

Lack of Patience

Another pitfall that new investors fall into is their lack of patience. When you are investing for the long-term, you cannot expect the returns to continuously be on the rise. There will be dips and peaks, and you'll have to learn how to ride it out until you see your returns coming in. A perfect example of this is the crazy crypto world. In a single year, we have watched Bitcoin rise to a peak of nearly $20,000 and then plummet to $6,000 in a matter of months. Patience will keep you from panicking and losing everything by exiting the market. Of course, no one knows if it is going to climb back up to the peak again or not, but the die-hard dedicated investors are willing to HODL until they have no other option. They are confident that cryptocurrency is here to stay and are willing to wait it out. It could take months, or it could take years, but those who are the most successful in such ventures are the ones who have the patience to wait for their rewards.

Not Doing Your Homework

Finally, not doing adequate research could become a major obstacle to your success. While there are many good investment opportunities, there are also many scams. If you fail to do your homework, you could end up giving your money away and losing it all in the process. It is important to understand the risks as much as the rewards. Don't take anyone's word for what they tell you, find out the facts for yourself and verify everything. Check and double-check before you make a final decision.

Learning how to invest is just like anything else you might want to get into. It takes a lot of up-front work, but if done correctly, you'll have a chance to build an incredible amount of wealth that will carry you into the future.

DOWNLOAD YOUR FREE BONUS:

77 Wealth Secrets

Go to: http://bit.ly/wealthsecrets77

Conclusion

Thank you for making it to the end of *Midlife Investing Strategies: A Comprehensive Guide to Investing in Your 40s*. Let's hope it was informative and able to provide you with all the tools you need to achieve your goals, whatever they may be.

Yes, investing can be scary, and getting started can be quite bumpy. In your 20s, you were just starting out in life; everything was an adventure. Your 30s were probably spent in search of something that could give meaning to your life. But at 40, you have finally settled into a lifestyle that makes you comfortable, and your concerns revolve around protecting it. If you're just now giving investing serious thought, there is no time like the present. You still have a bit of that youthful energy which they can use to get top earnings. That, in turn, can give you the bit of extra cash you could use to start investing.

By following the simple guidelines in this book, we hope we have taken much of the fear and anxiety out of the prospect. We hope that the advice we've given in this book is enough to get you excited about the future you hope to build and about what you can do to make it a reality. If you've learned anything at all from us here, it should be that it is never too late to start building your wealth and taking yourself on a journey toward financial independence.

Congratulations on starting a new chapter in your life! May it provide you with many happy and rewarding returns.

Finally, if you found this book useful in any way, a review on Amazon is always appreciated!

Printed in Great Britain
by Amazon